AF417952

"To Live Is Christ"

The Sermons of Pastor Charles H. Davis

Compiled and Edited By

Evangeline Davis Bibb

Copyright © 2021 Evangeline D. Bibb. The author retains sole copyright to this book.

**All Scripture quotations are from the Authorized Version of the King James Bible.*

**All hymns cited are in the public domain*

ISBN: 9798538729616

"I am crucified with Christ: nevertheless I live; yet not I, but Christ liveth in me: and the life which I now live in the flesh I live by the faith of the Son of God, who loved me, and gave himself for me."

Galatians 2:20

Table of Contents

Chapter 1: "The Message of the Cross"..1

Chapter 2: "A Question That Concerns All Humanity"........................13

Chapter 3: "The Worth of a Soul"..25

Chapter 4: "The Wondrous Gift of Salvation"........................39

Chapter 5: "Building For Eternity"..51

Chapter 6: "Stand Up and Be Counted"..61

Chapter 7: "Dead Flies In the Ointment"..69

Chapter 8: "A Call to Prayer"..77

Chapter 9: "The Harrows and Hosts of Hell"..87

Chapter 10: "Eternity's Insane Asylum"..95

Chapter 11: "Heaven- Where it is, What it will be Like, and Who will be There"..107

Chapter 12: "Are You Ready For Jesus To Come?"..123

Chapter 13: "Strangers and Gray Hairs"..137

Chapter 14: "What Time Is It?"..147

Chapter 15: "What Christmas Means to Me"..155

Pictures and Memories:..165

Introduction and Biographical Sketch

Charles H. Davis was born on October 20, 1936, in Plevna, Alabama. He was the child of Homer Earnest and Minnie Lou Davis, a humble farming family. He grew up in the hills of south central Tennessee. Charles was unchurched for some time as a small boy, until a concerned Christian invited him, along with his brother and sister, to a small Baptist church some miles from their family farm.

The Davis children- Wanda, Ray, and Charles -walked across the fields to the little church where they heard the precious story of Jesus Christ and His love. At the age of eleven, Charles and his family attended a revival meeting where they heard Pastor Raymond B. Kennedy preach the wondrous Gospel of Jesus Christ. There, in that humble meeting, the Holy Spirit of God moved in a mighty way to draw many souls to salvation and revival. Young Charles Davis was among those who trusted Jesus Christ as his Savior that night. Charles' entire family was transformed by the Spirit of God as a result of this meeting, and his parents became faithful believers and lifetime members of Donaldson Grove Baptist Church in Elora, Tennessee. Years later, Charles would meet and marry the granddaughter of Pastor Kennedy, the preacher whom God had used to make such an impact upon his life. Linda Burdett, the daughter of T.Z. and Sibyl Kennedy Burdett, became Charles' wife and faithful co-laborer in the ministry when they married on December 25, 1961. Linda served with and aided Charles in the work of the Lord through all their years of ministry in the churches. Linda was his wife, his secretary, his friend, and his co-laborer in the work of God, as well as the faithful mother of their children.

In his youth, as Charles was growing up and hearing the preaching of God's Word, he felt the clear call of the Holy Spirit to become a preacher of the Gospel. He began studying and preparing for the ministry and preached his first sermon at the age of sixteen. He was ordained to the Gospel ministry on September 6, 1959, at the age of twenty-two and accepted his first pastorate at that time.

Though surrendered to follow God's call, Charles still felt that something was missing in his life and ministry. After studying God's Word and reading some books on prayer and the work of the Holy Spirit, Charles felt a great burden to earnestly seek God's power upon his preaching and work for God. He determined to seek God's filling power through earnest prayer. When he finally emerged from the prayer closet, he came forth a broken, humble, and yielded servant of God, filled with the passion of His Savior "to seek and to save that which was lost," to compassionately serve God's people, and to preach with urgency the truth of God in the power of the Holy Ghost. After this experience of seeking the fullness of God's power, Bro. Davis commented, "My church thought that they had a new pastor." And so they did. They found in Bro. Charles Davis a man yielded to the working and leading of the Holy Spirit. Oh, what a difference this makes, for, as Christ told His own disciples, without Him, we can do nothing. Bro. Davis' ministry was marked by an unceasing desire to see souls come to salvation in Christ and to witness true revival among the sheep that God had entrusted to his care. How many times Bro. Charles' family and other believers saw him on his face, crying out to God for this continued power for himself and for others! How many times he wept over lost souls that he might win them to Jesus Christ! This was the work of God's grace in Bro. Davis' heart and the impelling motivation of his life.

In spite of all the busy work in ministry for the Lord, Bro. Charles always took time for his family. He taught them, by word and example, with patience and sincere love, to walk daily with the Savior who loved them so. God blessed Bro. Charles and his wife Linda with three daughters- Krista, Evangeline, and Aimee.

Bro. Davis went on to pastor churches in Illinois, Tennessee, Alabama, and Kentucky. Many souls were saved and Christians revived through the working of God's Spirit and the fervent preaching of the Word of God. Through the years, Bro. Charles had the privilege of preaching in many revival meetings. He also had the joy of taking the glorious Gospel of Jesus Christ to the regions beyond- to the continent of Africa, as well as to the islands of the Philippines -a place very near and dear to his heart. Many souls were saved and Christians revived through the earnest preaching of Pastor Charles Davis and other men of God who joined with him in these travels.

The sermons included in this collection are but a small sampling of the precious truths impressed upon Bro. Charles' heart by the Spirit of God as he earnestly prayed and pored over the Scriptures that were so precious to his soul. Though Bro. Davis regularly taught entire book studies of the Bible throughout his ministry, most of the sermons selected for this work are topical in nature. As much as possible, the editor has endeavored to draw from the exact words taken from Bro. Charles' own sermon notes, with some scriptures and explanations added for clarity and emphasis. We have included a hymn at the end of each sermon to further highlight the truths expounded in the messages.

Bro. Charles had an earnest desire to faithfully feed the flock of God over which the Lord had made him an overseer. To Bro. Davis, through all the labors and blessings of his life, love for Christ was the passion of his heart. He longed to see others grow in this same passion. It is our prayer that these sermons will draw Christians closer to Jesus Christ and bring lost souls to salvation.

2Co 5:14-15 "For the love of Christ constraineth us; because we thus judge, that if one died for all, then were all dead: And *that* he died for all, that they which live should not henceforth live unto themselves, but unto him which died for them, and rose again."

"He Lifted Me"

In loving-kindness Jesus came,

My soul in mercy to reclaim,

And from the depths of sin and shame

Through grace He lifted me.

From sinking sand He lifted me,

With tender hand He lifted me;

From shades of night to plains of light,

Oh, praise His Name, He lifted me!

He called me long before I heard,

Before my sinful heart was stirred,

But when I took Him at His word,

Forgiv'n, He lifted me.

From sinking sand He lifted me,

With tender hand He lifted me;

From shades of night to plains of light,

Oh, praise His Name, He lifted me!

His brow was pierced with many a thorn,

His hands by cruel nails were torn,

When from my guilt and grief, forlorn,

In love He lifted me.

From sinking sand He lifted me,

With tender hand He lifted me;

From shades of night to plains of light,

Oh, praise His Name, He lifted me!

Now on a higher plane I dwell,

And with my soul I know 'tis well;

Yet how or why, I cannot tell,

He should have lifted me.

From sinking sand He lifted me,

With tender hand He lifted me;

From shades of night to plains of light,

Oh, praise His Name, He lifted me!

-Charles H. Gabriel, 1905

"How then shall they call on him in whom they have not believed? And how shall they believe in him of whom they have not heard? And **how shall they hear without a preacher?** And how shall they preach, except they be sent? As it is written, How beautiful are the feet of them that preach the gospel of peace, and bring glad tidings of good things!"

Romans 10:14-15

Chapter 1:

"The Message of the Cross"
(Preached on March 27, 1994)

1Co 1:18-31 "For the preaching of the cross is to them that perish foolishness; but unto us which are saved it is the power of God. For it is written, I will destroy the wisdom of the wise, and will bring to nothing the understanding of the prudent. Where *is* the wise? where *is* the scribe? where *is* the disputer of this world? hath not God made foolish the wisdom of this world? For after that in the wisdom of God the world by wisdom knew not God, it pleased God by the foolishness of preaching to save them that believe. For the Jews require a sign, and the Greeks seek after wisdom: But we preach Christ crucified, unto the Jews a stumblingblock, and unto the Greeks foolishness; But unto them which are called, both Jews and Greeks, Christ the power of God, and the wisdom of God. Because the foolishness of God is wiser than men; and the weakness of God is stronger than men. For ye see your calling, brethren, how that not many wise men after the flesh, not many mighty, not many noble, *are called*: But God hath chosen the foolish things of the world to confound the wise; and God hath chosen the weak things of the world to confound the things which are mighty; And base things of the world, and things which are despised, hath God chosen, *yea*, and things which are not, to bring to nought things that are: That no flesh should glory in his presence. But of him are ye in Christ Jesus, who of God is made unto us wisdom, and righteousness, and sanctification, and redemption: That, according as it is written, He that glorieth, let him glory in the Lord."

The cross was no mistake, no surprise, no colossal blunder. The cross was the fulfillment of God's purpose in sending His Son into the world. It was the supreme reason for Christ leaving the portals of glory and taking upon Himself the likeness of man. Jesus did not die as a martyr to a noble cause or as just a worthy example for others to follow. He died as a substitute for a sinful world. His death was in keeping with His life, His teachings, and God's eternal plan to "bring many sons to glory" (Heb. 2:10).Jesus said, "Except a corn of wheat fall into the ground and die, it abideth alone: but if it die, it bringeth forth much fruit" (Joh. 12:24). He declared, "And I, if I be lifted up from the earth, will draw all *men* unto me" (Joh. 12:32).

The lost world fails to understand why the Church loves the cross and glories in it. They have not yet been touched by its power and constrained by its love. They have not yet come to know its message. But the cross has a glorious message that desperately needs to be heard by the world and by the Church; for even as the world has not heard and understood the message, the Church far too often has not fully embraced it.

The Love of God for a Lost World

The Cross is God's Love Message to Humanity:

Joh 3:16 "For God so loved the world, that he gave his only begotten Son, that whosoever believeth in him should not perish, but have everlasting life."

Ro 5:8 "But God commendeth his love toward us, in that, while we were yet sinners, Christ died for us."

The cross says that God loves you. Many things happen in this life that we do not understand. There are times when God does not seem to make sense to us. But the cross reassures us of His love. The cross shows the great value that God has placed upon our eternal souls.

The Cross Reveals that God Goes to Great Lengths to Save Sinners:

Human souls are God's primary concern, and human souls should be our concern as well. God gave His all to save sinners. What are we giving of ourselves to keep people out of hell?

The Cross Tells us that there is a Hell- An Eternal, Burning Hell:

Mr 9:43-48 "And if thy hand offend thee, cut it off: it is better for thee to enter into life maimed, than having two hands to go into hell, into the fire that never shall be quenched: Where their worm dieth not, and the fire is not quenched. And if thy foot offend thee, cut it off: it is better for thee to enter halt into life, than having two feet to be cast into hell, into the fire that never shall be quenched: Where their worm dieth not, and the fire is not quenched. And if thine eye offend thee, pluck it out: it is better for thee to enter into the kingdom of God with one eye, than having two eyes to be cast into hell fire Where their worm dieth not, and the fire is not quenched."

Mt 25:41 "Then shall he say also unto them on the left hand, Depart from me, ye cursed, into everlasting fire, prepared for the devil and his angels:"

Re 20:11-15 "And I saw a great white throne, and him that sat on it, from whose face the earth and the heaven fled away; and there was found no place for them. And I saw the dead, small and great, stand before God; and the books were opened: and another book was opened, which is *the book* of life: and the dead were judged out of those things which were written in the books, according to their works. And the sea gave up the dead which were in it; and death and hell delivered up the dead which were in them: and they were judged every man according to their works. And death and hell were cast into the lake of fire. This is the second death. And whosoever was not found written in the book of life was cast into the lake of fire."

The Cross Tells Us that God's Love is Unconditional:

God loves you as you are:

Ro 5:6-8 "For when we were yet without strength, in due time Christ died for the ungodly. For scarcely for a righteous man will one die: yet peradventure for a good man some would even dare to die. But God commendeth his love toward us, in that, while we were yet sinners, Christ died for us."

God loves all sinners equally:

2Pe 3:9 "The Lord is not slack concerning his promise, as some men count slackness; but is longsuffering to us-ward, not willing that any should perish, but that all should come to repentance."

God loves all sinners- drunkards, adulterers, prostitutes, child molesters, murderers, thieves, the morally perverse, the religious, the atheistic, rich and poor, weak and powerful- all races, and all creeds of men -God loves lost sinners, and longs to see them come to repentance and salvation in Jesus Christ. Jesus Christ paid the sin debt for all sinners:

1Jo 2:1-2 "My little children, these things write I unto you, that ye sin not. And if any man sin, we have an advocate with the Father, Jesus Christ the righteous: And he is the propitiation for our sins: and not for ours only, **but also for *the sins of* the whole world."**

God loved you enough to give His own Son to save you:

Joh 3:17 "For God sent not his Son into the world to condemn the world; but that the world through him might be saved."

1Jo 4:14 "And we have seen and do testify that the Father sent the Son *to be* the Saviour of the world."

God loved you enough to forgive and to pardon you:

Col 1:12-14 "Giving thanks unto the Father, which hath made us meet to be partakers of the inheritance of the saints in light: Who hath delivered us from the power of darkness, and hath translated *us* into the kingdom of his dear Son: **In whom we have redemption through his blood, *even* the forgiveness of sins:"**

The Cross Reveals that God's Love is Constant, Unchanging, and Immeasurable:

Ro 8:32, 37-39 "He that spared not his own Son, but delivered him up for us all, how shall he not with him also freely give us all things..."Nay, in all these things we are more than conquerors through him that loved us. For I am persuaded, that neither death, nor life, nor angels, nor principalities, nor powers, nor things present, nor things to come, Nor height, nor depth, nor any other creature, shall be able to separate us from the love of God, which is in Christ Jesus our Lord."

The Cross Reveals That Sin is Unspeakably Bad:

God is holy and must punish sin.

Ro 6:23 "For the wages of sin *is* death; but the gift of God *is* eternal life through Jesus Christ our Lord."

Sin has brought ruin and death to all of creation:

Ro 5:12 "Wherefore, as by one man sin entered into the world, and death by sin; and so death passed upon all men, for that all have sinned:"

Sin has separated man from God.

Sin has brought condemnation:

Joh 3:18 "He that believeth on him is not condemned: but he that believeth not is condemned already, because he hath not believed in the name of the only begotten Son of God."

Sin has destroyed peace and love:

Isa 48:22 "*There is* no peace, saith the LORD, unto the wicked."

Sin's cost is unspeakably terrible- it is eternal:

Mt 25:41 "Then shall he say also unto them on the left hand, Depart from me, ye cursed, into everlasting fire, prepared for the devil and his angels:"

Sin cost God a terrible price. He spared not His own Son, but gave Him up for us all:

Ro 8:32 "He that spared not his own Son, but delivered him up for us all, how shall he not with him also freely give us all things?"

Php 2:5-8 "Let this mind be in you, which was also in Christ Jesus: Who, being in the form of God, thought it not robbery to be equal with God: But made himself of no reputation, and took upon him the form of a servant, and was made in the likeness of men: And being found in fashion as a man, he humbled himself, and became obedient unto death, even the death of the cross."

The Cross Demonstrates for Us How Terrible It Is to Be Lost, for it gives us a Preview of Hell through Christ's Sufferings:

Jesus Christ suffered all the torments of hell on our behalf:

Mr 15:33-34 "And when the sixth hour was come, there was darkness over the whole land until the ninth hour. And at the ninth hour Jesus cried with a loud voice, saying, Eloi, Eloi, lama sabachthani? which is, being interpreted, My God, my God, why hast thou forsaken me?"

2Co 5:21 "For he hath made him *to be* sin for us, who knew no sin; that we might be made the righteousness of God in him."

As Christians, The Cross Shows Us That We Can Be Free:

Free From Condemnation:

We are justified through His blood:

Ro 5:9 "Much more then, being now justified by his blood, we shall be saved from wrath through him."

Free to Be Complete in Jesus:

Christ has set us free from sin's dominion:

Ro 6:14 "For sin shall not have dominion over you: for ye are not under the law, but under grace."

Christ has loosed us from the tyranny of self:

Ga 2:20 "I am crucified with Christ: nevertheless I live; yet not I, but Christ liveth in me: and the life which I now live in the flesh I live by the faith of the Son of God, who loved me, and gave himself for me."

Free to Obey God and to Grow in the Likeness of Jesus Christ:

Ga 5:1 "Stand fast therefore in the liberty wherewith Christ hath made us free, and be not entangled again with the yoke of bondage."

We don't have to strive to make ourselves acceptable to God. We are accepted in Christ:

Eph 1:6-7 "To the praise of the glory of his grace, wherein he hath made us accepted in the beloved. In whom we have redemption through his blood, the forgiveness of sins, according to the riches of his grace;"

Col 1:12 "Giving thanks unto the Father, which hath made us meet to be partakers of the inheritance of the saints in light:"

1Jo 3:1 "Behold, what manner of love the Father hath bestowed upon us, that we should be called the sons of God..."

We are free to serve God because we love Him:

Ro 5:5 "And hope maketh not ashamed; because the love of God is shed abroad in our hearts by the Holy Ghost which is given unto us."

1Jo 4:19 "We love him, because he first loved us."

We are free from guilt. We are forgiven in Christ:

Col 1:13-14 "Who hath delivered us from the power of darkness, and hath translated *us* into the kingdom of his dear Son: In whom we have redemption through his blood, *even* the forgiveness of sins:"

We need to confess our sins to God and repent of sin with broken hearts to keep in sweet fellowship with Him:

1Jo 1:7-9 "But if we walk in the light, as he is in the light, we have fellowship one with another, and the blood of Jesus Christ his Son cleanseth us from all sin. If we say that we have no sin, we deceive ourselves, and the truth is not in us. If we confess our sins, he is faithful and just to forgive us *our* sins, and to cleanse us from all unrighteousness."

We need to yield our lives to God even unto death because we love and desire to please Him:

Ro 12:1-2 "I beseech you therefore, brethren, by the mercies of God, that ye present your bodies a living sacrifice, holy, acceptable unto God, *which is* your reasonable service. And be not conformed to this world: but be ye transformed by the renewing of your mind, that ye may prove what *is* that good, and acceptable, and perfect, will of God."

Free to Live the Resurrected Life:

-To be filled with the fullness of God

-To receive Christ's sufficiency and respond to His grace

-To love and forgive one another

-To give ourselves in boldness to witness and share His love

Bondage Comes When We Refuse to Submit to God's Truth:

As Christians, we are often bound by our own feelings, attitudes and behaviors-pride, bitterness, lack of forgiveness, inferiority, intimidation, worthlessness, superiority, over-sensitivity, hopelessness, rejection, anger, strife, malice, adultery, drunkenness, stubbornness, rebellion, etc. All these things are a result of a failure to surrender to the truth of God and accept what we are in Christ. Such rejection and refusal causes us to be in bondage to self and sin:

Eph 4:30-32 "And grieve not the holy Spirit of God, whereby ye are sealed unto the day of redemption. Let all bitterness, and wrath, and anger, and clamour, and evil speaking, be put away from you, with all malice: And be ye kind one to another, tenderhearted, forgiving one another, even as God for Christ's sake hath forgiven you."

Many believers are enslaved- dominated by selfish desires.

God's Remedy For the Christian is the Cross and Obedience to God's Word:

The cross frees us as we die to self and surrender to Christ's life within. As we respond to His love and yield to His grace, He gives us power to live a life pleasing to Him through obedience to the Word of God. The answer for the Christian is still the power of the cross. Christ died for us that we might live for Him:

Ga 2:20 "I am crucified with Christ: nevertheless I live; yet not I, but Christ liveth in me: and the life which I now live in the flesh I live by the faith of the Son of God, who loved me, and gave himself for me."

The flesh is the old nature- what we are in Adam. But for the Christian, the old nature has been crucified, judged, and condemned at the cross.

The path to victory for the Christian is for self to be renounced, Christ to be enthroned, and Jesus Christ to be everything. The great hindrance to salvation, sanctification, and service is self. But there is victory in Jesus Christ if we are willing to accept the cross of Christ as our own, and live the resurrected life that Christ's power provides.

Ro 6:11-14 "Likewise reckon ye also yourselves to be dead indeed unto sin, but alive unto God through Jesus Christ our Lord. Let not sin therefore reign in your mortal body, that ye should obey it in the lusts thereof. Neither yield ye your members *as* instruments of unrighteousness unto sin: but yield yourselves unto God, as those that are alive from the dead, and your members *as* instruments of righteousness unto God. For sin shall not have dominion over you: for ye are not under the law, but under grace."

There is victory in Christ and in His cross!

"The Old Rugged Cross"

On a hill far away stood an old rugged cross,

The emblem of suff'ring and shame;

And I love that old cross where the Dearest and Best

For a world of lost sinners was slain.

So I'll cherish the old rugged cross,

Till my trophies at last I lay down;

I will cling to the old rugged cross,

And exchange it someday for a crown.

Oh, that old rugged cross, so despised by the world,

Has a wondrous attraction for me;

For the dear Lamb of God left His glory above

To bear it to dark Calvary.

So I'll cherish the old rugged cross,

Till my trophies at last I lay down;

I will cling to the old rugged cross,

And exchange it someday for a crown.

In that old rugged cross, stained with blood so divine,

A wondrous beauty I see,

For 'twas on that old cross Jesus suffered and died,

To pardon and sanctify me.

So I'll cherish the old rugged cross,

Till my trophies at last I lay down;

I will cling to the old rugged cross,

And exchange it someday for a crown.

To the old rugged cross I will ever be true;

Its shame and reproach gladly bear;

Then He'll call me someday to my home far away,

Where His glory forever I'll share.

So I'll cherish the old rugged cross,

Till my trophies at last I lay down;

I will cling to the old rugged cross,

And exchange it someday for a crown.

-George Bennard, 1913

To Live is Christ

Chapter 2

"A Question That Concerns All Humanity"
(Preached on October 8, 1989)

Job 25:4 "How then can man be justified with God? or how can he be clean *that is* born of a woman?"

I want to speak to you today on the subject, "A Question that Concerns All Humanity." It is a question found in the oldest book in the Bible, written nearly four thousand years ago. Yet, it is as pertinent and pressing today as it was then. The question is that which we have already read in this passage, "How then can a man be justified with God?" The importance of this question demands a plain and heart-satisfying answer. This plain and satisfying answer can only be found upon the pages of God's Word. Other answers are wholly unsatisfactory since they do not deal with the primary issues- the sinfulness of man and the holiness of God. As we thus focus upon this truth, we will center our attention primarily upon Romans chapters 3-5. In answering this question, I will ask and answer from the Bible three other questions:

<u>Who Needs to be Justified?</u>

All are Under Sin:

Ro 3:9 "What then? are we better *than they*? No, in no wise: for we have before proved both Jews and Gentiles, that they are all under sin;"

None are Righteous:

Ro 3:10 "As it is written, There is none righteous, no, not one:"

All are Gone Out of the Way:

Ro 3:12 "They are all gone out of the way, they are together become unprofitable; there is none that doeth good, no, not one."

The Entire World is Guilty Before God:

Ro 3:19 "Now we know that what things soever the law saith, it saith to them who are under the law: that every mouth may be stopped, and all the world may become guilty before God."

All are in Need of Justification:

Ro 3:21-23 "But now the righteousness of God without the law is manifested, being witnessed by the law and the prophets; Even the righteousness of God *which is* by faith of Jesus Christ unto all and upon all them that believe: for there is no difference: For all have sinned, and come short of the glory of God;"

There is no difference- all have sinned. We are not only sinners by nature, we are sinners by choice.

What is Justification?

Justification Means "to Declare Righteous":

Ro 5:18 -19 "Therefore as by the offence of one *judgment came* upon all men to condemnation; even so by the righteousness of one *the free gift came* upon all men unto justification of life. For as by one man's disobedience many were made sinners, so by the obedience of one shall many be made righteous."

Justification is an Act which Only God Can Perform:

Ro 8:33 "...*It is* God that justifieth."

God alone can justify sinners, for it is His law that has been broken. Sin is against God. He is the one who has been offended.

Justification is for the Ungodly:

Ro 5:6 "For when we were yet without strength, in due time Christ died for the ungodly."

Ro 5:8 "But God commendeth his love toward us, in that, while we were yet sinners, Christ died for us."

Ro 4:5 "But to him that worketh not, but believeth on him that justifieth the ungodly, his faith is counted for righteousness."

God justifies the ungodly. He saves sinners who will repent before God and believe on His Son. A wonderful example of how God justifies the ungodly sinner who is willing to cast himself upon God's mercy is found in a story that Jesus Christ told in Luke 18. In this illustration, Christ clearly pointed out that man can never justify himself before God. God alone is the justifier of the ungodly sinner who calls in faith upon Him:

Lu 18:9-14 "And he spake this parable unto certain which trusted in themselves that they were righteous, and despised others: Two men went up into the temple to pray; the one a Pharisee, and the other a publican. The Pharisee stood and prayed thus with himself, God, I thank thee, that I am not as other men *are*, extortioners, unjust, adulterers, or even as this publican. I fast twice in the week, I give tithes of all that I possess. And the publican, standing afar off, would not lift up so much as *his* eyes unto heaven, but smote upon his breast, saying, God be merciful to me a sinner. I tell you, this man went down to his house **justified** *rather* than the other: for every one that exalteth himself shall be abased; and he that humbleth himself shall be exalted."

It is Impossible for Man to Justify Himself:

The law cannot save us, for we are sinners before God:

Ro 3:20 "Therefore by the deeds of the law there shall no flesh be justified in his sight: for by the law *is* the knowledge of sin."

Man's "goodness" is unacceptable before God:

Ro 3:12 "They are all gone out of the way, they are together become unprofitable; there is none that doeth good, no, not one."

A Biblical Illustration of Justification by Faith- Abraham:

The Old Testament patriarch, Abraham, was <u>not</u> justified before God by his good deeds:

Ro 4:1-5 "What shall we say then that Abraham our father, as pertaining to the flesh, hath found? For if Abraham were justified by works, he hath *whereof* to glory; but not before God. For what saith the scripture? Abraham **believed** God, and it was counted unto him for righteousness. Now to him that worketh is the reward not reckoned of grace, but of debt. But to him that worketh not, but believeth on him that justifieth the ungodly, his faith is counted for righteousness."

Abraham was accepted- declared righteous -by faith in God's truth.

Another Biblical Illustration of Justification- the high priest, Joshua:

In the book of Zechariah, the prophet saw a vision of Joshua, the high priest, standing before the LORD. He was clothed with filthy garments, and Satan was accusing him before the LORD:

Zec 3:1-5 "And he shewed me Joshua the high priest standing before the angel of the LORD, and Satan standing at his right hand to resist him. And the LORD said unto Satan, The LORD rebuke thee, O Satan; even the LORD that hath chosen Jerusalem rebuke thee: *is* not this a brand plucked out of the fire? Now Joshua was clothed with filthy garments, and stood before the angel. And he answered and spake unto those that stood before him, saying, **Take away the filthy garments from him. And unto him he said, Behold, I have caused thine iniquity to pass from thee, and I will clothe thee with change of raiment.** And I said, Let them set a fair mitre upon his head. So they set a fair mitre upon his head, and clothed him with garments. And the angel of the LORD stood by."

In this precious passage, the LORD God takes away the filthy garments from Joshua. He cleanses him from his iniquity, and clothes him with new garments, and crowns him with glory and beauty. This is a beautiful picture of how God justifies the sinner. The atoning blood of Jesus stands between the justified sinner and holy God, making him acceptable before God. God Himself, in the Person of Jesus Christ, stands between His people and every accusation that may be brought against them. At salvation, God takes our sin and iniquity away and clothes us in the righteousness of Jesus Christ Himself:

2Co 5:21 "For he hath made him *to be* sin for us, who knew no sin; that we might be made the righteousness of God in him."

Php 3:9 "And be found in him, not having mine own righteousness, which is of the law, but that which is through the faith of Christ, the righteousness which is of God by faith:"

Ro 8:33-34 "Who shall lay any thing to the charge of God's elect? *It is* God that justifieth. Who *is* he that condemneth? *It is* Christ that died, yea rather, that is risen again, who is even at the right hand of God, who also maketh intercession for us."

Justification is the Clearing of the Guilty:

To Be Justified is to Have Our Sins Forgiven:

Ro 4:7-8 "*Saying,* Blessed *are* they whose iniquities are forgiven, and whose sins are covered. Blessed *is* the man to whom the Lord will not impute sin."

When we are justified, our sins are no longer counted against us. Our guilt is forever removed.

This same truth is stated in Acts 13:

Ac 13:38-39 "Be it known unto you therefore, men *and* brethren, that through this man is preached unto you the forgiveness of sins: And by him all that believe are justified from all things, from which ye could not be justified by the law of Moses."

To Be Justified is to Be Reckoned Righteous:

Ro 4:9 "*Cometh* this blessedness then upon the circumcision *only*, or upon the uncircumcision also? for we say that faith was reckoned to Abraham for righteousness."

Another Biblical Illustration- Cain and Abel:

Before God can accept our works, He must be able to accept our person. This only possible through the atoning blood of God's acceptable sacrifice:

Ge 4:1-5 "And Adam knew Eve his wife; and she conceived, and bare Cain, and said, I have gotten a man from the LORD. And she again bare his brother Abel. And Abel was a keeper of sheep, but Cain was a tiller of the ground. And in process of time it came to pass, that Cain brought of the fruit of the ground an offering unto the LORD. And Abel, he also brought of the firstlings of his flock and of the fat thereof. And the LORD had respect unto Abel and to his offering: But unto Cain and to his offering he had not respect. And Cain was very wroth, and his countenance fell."

"...the LORD had respect unto Abel and to his offering: But unto Cain and to his offering he had not respect." What made the difference? Faith in the shed blood prescribed by God is what made Abel and his offering acceptable before God. It was a blood offering brought by faith in the truth and commandments of God.

To Be Justified is to be Reconciled to God and to be Spared from Wrath:

Ro 5:9-10 "Much more then, being now justified by his blood, we shall be saved from wrath through him. For if, when we were enemies, we were reconciled to God by the death of his Son, much more, being reconciled, we shall be saved by his life."

God alone could deliver the sinner from the eternal wages of sin. He did it through the sacrifice of His own Son, Jesus Christ. Jesus died in the place of sinners and took our eternal punishment when He shed His blood upon the cross of Calvary:

Joh 3:16 "For God so loved the world, that he gave his only begotten Son, that whosoever believeth in him **should not perish**, but have everlasting life."

To Be Justified is to have Peace with God:

Ro 5:1 "Therefore being justified by faith, we have peace with God through our Lord Jesus Christ:"

When Adam sinned, he had no peace:

Ge 3:9-10 "And the LORD God called unto Adam, and said unto him, Where *art* thou? And he said, I heard thy voice in the garden, and I was afraid, because I *was* naked; and I hid myself."

Sin robs us of peace; but justification brings peace because our sins are blotted out. Our condemnation is removed:

Ro 8:1 "*There is* therefore now no condemnation to them which are in Christ Jesus, who walk not after the flesh, but after the Spirit."

<u>How Is Justification Possible?</u>

Ro 3:23-26 "For all have sinned, and come short of the glory of God; Being justified freely **by his grace through the redemption that is in Christ Jesus**: Whom God hath set forth *to be* a propitiation through faith in his blood, to declare his righteousness for the remission of sins that are past, through the forbearance of God; To declare, *I say*, at this time his righteousness: that he might be just, and the justifier of him which believeth in Jesus."

Justification Was Made Possible by Jesus Christ's Death and Resurrection:

Ro 4:24-25 "But for us also, to whom it shall be imputed, if we believe on him that raised up Jesus our Lord from the dead; Who was delivered for our offences, and was raised again for our justification."

Jesus was "delivered" for our offenses:

Jesus Christ was given up as a sacrifice for our sins. This is **substitution**. Christ was our substitute. We are all sinners justly condemned by a holy God. Jesus took our place. God's judgment and just punishment fell upon Him. Jesus Christ paid the price in full for our sins. When we come to Christ, trusting His sacrifice on our behalf by faith, our condemnation is removed. Christ became sin for us. He bore our sins in His own body on the tree. Our sins were "imputed" to Christ. They were put on His account, and He paid the debt we owed:

1Pe 2:24-25 "Who his own self bare our sins in his own body on the tree, that we, being dead to sins, should live unto righteousness: by whose stripes ye were healed. For ye were as sheep going astray; but are now returned unto the Shepherd and Bishop of your souls."

Jesus Christ was raised from the dead "for our justification":

God placed our sins upon Jesus- the righteous, sinless One-that our penalty of sin might be paid. Then, God raised Christ up from the dead "for our justification." The resurrection was the unquestionable proof that the sin debt was forever settled. Now, because of Christ's death, burial, and resurrection, justification is available for any sinner who will receive it by faith in what Jesus Christ did on our behalf.

Justification is Made Possible by the Imputation of God:

Ro 4:5-8 "But to him that worketh not, but believeth on him that justifieth the ungodly, his faith is counted for righteousness. Even as David also describeth the blessedness of the man, unto whom God imputeth righteousness without works, *Saying*, Blessed *are* they whose iniquities are forgiven, and whose sins are covered. Blessed *is* the man to whom the Lord will not impute sin."

Justification is an Act of God:

As the righteous Judge, He declares righteous the sinner who believes on His Son, Jesus Christ:

Joh 3:36 "He that believeth on the Son hath everlasting life: and he that believeth not the Son shall not see life; but the wrath of God abideth on him."

Justification is Possible Only through the Blood of Jesus Christ:

1Pe 1:18-19 "Forasmuch as ye know that ye were not redeemed with corruptible things, *as* silver and gold, from your vain conversation *received* by tradition from your fathers; But with the precious blood of Christ, as of a lamb without blemish and without spot:"

It Must Be Received By Faith:

Ro 3:25-26 "Whom God hath set forth *to be* a propitiation through faith in his blood, to declare his righteousness for the remission of sins that are past, through the forbearance of God; To declare, *I say*, at this time his righteousness: that he might be just, and the justifier of him which believeth in Jesus."

Ro 5:1 "Therefore being justified by faith, we have peace with God through our Lord Jesus Christ:"

Won't you accept this free gift of justification by faith in Jesus Christ?

"There is a Fountain"

There is a fountain filled with blood,

Drawn from Immanuel's veins,

And sinners plunged beneath that flood

Lose all their guilty stains:

Lose all their guilty stains,

Lose all their guilty stains;

And sinners plunged beneath that flood

Lose all their guilty stains.

The dying thief rejoiced to see

That fountain in His day;

And there may I, though vile as he,

Wash all my sins away:

Wash all my sins away,

Wash all my sins away;

And there may I, though vile as he,

Wash all my sins away.

Dear dying Lamb, Thy precious blood

Shall never lose its pow'r,

Till all the ransomed church of God

Be saved, to sin no more:

Be saved, to sin no more,

Be saved, to sin no more;

Till all the ransomed church of God

Be saved, to sin no more.

E'er since by faith I saw the stream

Thy flowing wounds supply,

Redeeming love has been my theme,

And shall be till I die:

And shall be till I die,

And shall be till I die;

Redeeming love has been my theme,

And shall be till I die.

When this poor, lisping, stamm'ring tongue

Lies silent in the grave,

Then in a nobler, sweeter song,

I'll sing Thy pow'r to save:

I'll sing Thy pow'r to save,

I'll sing Thy pow'r to save;

Then in a nobler, sweeter song,

I'll sing Thy pow'r to save."

-*William Cowper, 1772*

Chapter 3

"The Worth of a Soul"
(Preached on June 13, 1993)

What is the most valuable thing in the universe? Someone would likely say, "Gold!" Someone else might suggest diamonds, or, perhaps, plutonium? There are many things much more valuable than any of these. Air? Water? Health? Food? Freedom? These are things beyond value. They are necessary to life and happiness. Yet, there is something of greater worth than even these. What is it? It is your eternal soul. Today, I want us to measure the worth of a soul.

Jesus spoke of the inestimable value of a human soul:

Mr 8:34-37 "And when he had called the people *unto him* with his disciples also, he said unto them, Whosoever will come after me, let him deny himself, and take up his cross, and follow me. For whosoever will save his life shall lose it; but whosoever shall lose his life for my sake and the gospel's, the same shall save it. For what shall it profit a man, if he shall gain the whole world, and lose his own soul? Or what shall a man give in exchange for his soul?"

<u>Men Often Place Great Value on Lesser Things to the Neglect of Their Souls:</u>

Some examples of this include:

Judas Iscariot:

Judas was a disciple of Jesus Christ. He was one of the twelve personally selected by the Savior. He heard Jesus' words. He saw Christ's mighty works, yet, Judas was never saved. He did not believe on Jesus Christ, the Savior and Lord. He was consumed by a love of money:

Joh 12:4-6 "Then saith one of his disciples, Judas Iscariot, Simon's *son*, which should betray him, Why was not this ointment sold for three hundred pence, and given to the poor? This he said, not that he cared for the poor; but because he was a thief, and had the bag, and bare what was put therein."

Judas put more value upon money than upon his soul. Of Judas, Jesus said:

Joh 6:63-64, 70-71 "It is the spirit that quickeneth; the flesh profiteth nothing: the words that I speak unto you, *they* are spirit, and *they* are life. **But there are some of you that believe not.** For Jesus knew from the beginning who they were that believed not, and who should betray him...Jesus answered them, Have not I chosen you twelve, and one of you is a devil? He spake of Judas Iscariot *the son* of Simon: for he it was that should betray him, being one of the twelve."

Rich, Young Ruler:

Another example of one who valued things more than his soul is found in Luke 18:

Lu 18:18 -25 "And a certain ruler asked him, saying, Good Master, what shall I do to inherit eternal life? And Jesus said unto him, Why callest thou me good? none *is* good, save one, *that is*, God. Thou knowest the commandments, Do not commit adultery, Do not kill, Do not steal, Do not bear false witness, Honour thy father and thy mother. And he said, All these have I kept from my youth up. Now when Jesus heard these things, he said unto him, Yet lackest thou one thing: sell all that thou hast, and distribute unto the poor, and thou shalt have treasure in heaven: and come, follow me. And when he heard this, he was very sorrowful: for he was very rich. And when Jesus saw that he was very sorrowful, he said, How hardly shall they that have riches enter into the kingdom of God! For it is easier for a camel to go through a needle's eye, than for a rich man to enter into the kingdom of God."

This young man thought he was good enough to earn eternal life. He did not see that he was covetous and loved riches more than his own soul.

The Rich Fool:

Another biblical example is found in Luke 12:

Lu 12:15-21 "And he said unto them, Take heed, and beware of covetousness: for a man's life consisteth not in the abundance of the things which he possesseth. And he spake a parable unto them, saying, The ground of a certain rich man brought forth plentifully: And he thought within himself, saying, What shall I do, because I have no room where to bestow my fruits? And he said, This will I do: I will pull down my barns, and build greater; and there will I bestow all my fruits and my goods. And I will say to my soul, Soul, thou hast much goods laid up for many years; take thine ease, eat, drink, *and* be merry. But God said unto him, *Thou* fool, this night thy soul shall be required of thee: then whose shall those things be, which thou hast provided? So *is* he that layeth up treasure for himself, and is not rich toward God."

Then, we see two other examples who heard the preaching and testimony of the Apostle Paul:

Governor Felix:

Ac 24:24-26 "And after certain days, when Felix came with his wife Drusilla, which was a Jewess, he sent for Paul, and heard him concerning the faith in Christ. And as he reasoned of righteousness, temperance, and judgment to come, Felix trembled, and answered, Go thy way for this time; when I have a convenient season, I will call for thee. He hoped also that money should have been given him of Paul, that he might loose him: wherefore he sent for him the oftener, and communed with him."

King Agrippa:

Ac 26:27-28 "King Agrippa, believest thou the prophets? I know that thou believest. Then Agrippa said unto Paul, Almost thou persuadest me to be a Christian."

All of these biblical examples valued something- popularity, position, pleasure, possessions -more than their eternal soul, and all to their everlasting doom.

The Worth of a Soul is Seen in the Dedication Some Have Had in Winning The Lost:

The Concern of Paul, the Apostle:

Ro 9:1-3 "I say the truth in Christ, I lie not, my conscience also bearing me witness in the Holy Ghost, That I have great heaviness and continual sorrow in my heart. For I could wish that myself were accursed from Christ for my brethren, my kinsmen according to the flesh:"

Paul showed that concern by a sacrificial life:

Ac 20:24 "But none of these things move me, neither count I my life dear unto myself, so that I might finish my course with joy, and the ministry, which I have received of the Lord Jesus, to testify the gospel of the grace of God."

The Concern of Other Christians in Recent History:

David Brainerd:

The missionary, David Brainerd, labored earnestly for the souls of native American Indians in the early days of colonial America. He labored under terrible hardship and trials, travelling long miles on horseback in rain, snow, and all types of weather to reach the remote villages of native tribes. God had put this great burden upon his heart to reach these people living in spiritual darkness. Sick and weak in body, David Brainerd died at the age of twenty-nine. His sense of the value of a soul was expressed in a life literally poured out for the souls of men and in his own words taken from his own diary:

"I care not where I live, or what hardships I go through, so that I can but gain souls to Christ. While I am asleep, I dream of these things; as soon as I awake, the first thing I think of is this great work. All my desire is the conversion of sinners, and all my hope is in God." (*The Life and Diary of David Brainerd,* by David Brainerd, 1749)

William Booth:

William Booth was the founder of the ministry known as The Salvation Army. He founded this ministry out of an earnest desire to reach the poor and destitute with the saving Gospel of Jesus Christ. In his own words, we find his great passion for the souls of men. He said,

"Some men's ambition is art. Some men's ambition is fame. Some men's ambition is gold. My ambition is the souls of men."

Charles H. Spurgeon:

The famed preacher of the nineteenth century, Charles Spurgeon, was once given an offer to come and deliver fifty lectures in fifty days in the major cities of the United States. The promised remuneration for his lecture tour was one thousand dollars a day for each day of the tour- $50,000 in fifty days of speaking engagements. Spurgeon refused the offer, saying, "I can do better. I will stay in London and try to save fifty souls."

Charles Spurgeon had a proper sense of the worth of souls.

John Harper:

John Harper is a lesser known character in history, but oh, what an understanding he had of the worth of an eternal soul. In the early 1900s, Bro. Harper, a godly pastor from Scotland, was called to be pastor of the Moody Church in Chicago, Illinois. In the providence of God, Bro. Harper happened to be one of the passengers aboard the ill-fated British ocean liner, the *Titanic*. Bro. John Harper was among the victims who died in the sinking of the Titanic. But the story of John Harper's life does not end there. When the *Titanic* struck the iceberg that eventually sent her to the bottom of the ocean, Bro. John Harper was leaning against the rail of the ship talking to a young man, urging him to receive Christ. Four years later, another young man, a survivor of the tragedy, rose in a meeting to give this testimony:

"I am a survivor of the *Titanic*. When I was drifting alone on a spar that awful night, the tide brought Mr. John Harper along, also drifting on a piece of wreck near me. 'Man, he said, 'are you saved?' 'No,' I said. 'I am not.' He replied, 'Believe on the Lord Jesus Christ and thou shalt be saved.' The waves bore him away: but strange to say, brought him back a little later, and he said, 'Are you saved now?' 'No,' I said. 'I cannot honestly say that I am.' He said, 'Believe on the Lord Jesus Christ, and thou shalt be saved.' And shortly after, he went down; and there, alone in the night, and with two miles of water under me, I believed. I am John Harper's last convert." (Editor: This story can be found online at https://middletownbiblechurch.org/helpseek/titanjh.htm; "The Little Known Story of John Harper").

The Worth of a Soul Must be Measured by the Sacrifice of Jesus:

Christ's Sacrifice in Becoming a Man:

Php 2:5 -7 "Let this mind be in you, which was also in Christ Jesus: Who, being in the form of God, thought it not robbery to be equal with God: But made himself of no reputation, and took upon him the form of a servant, and was made in the likeness of men:"

Jesus left Heaven's glory- a place of peace, plenty, worship, and love -to come to earth to be "despised and rejected of men; a man of sorrows, and acquainted with grief..." (Isa. 53:3) -all to save helpless sinners.

Christ's Sacrificial Life:

Jesus gave up the riches of glory to become poor and afflicted for our sakes:

2Co 8:9 "For ye know the grace of our Lord Jesus Christ, that, though he was rich, yet for your sakes he became poor, that ye through his poverty might be rich."

Christ's Suffering Before the Cross:

For the sake of souls, Jesus suffered the agony in the Garden of Gethsemane and the mock trials before the Jews, Pilate, and Herod:

Lu 22:41 -44 "And he was withdrawn from them about a stone's cast, and kneeled down, and prayed, Saying, Father, if thou be willing, remove this cup from me: nevertheless not my will, but thine, be done. And there appeared an angel unto him from heaven, strengthening him. And being in an agony he prayed more earnestly: and his sweat was as it were great drops of blood falling down to the ground."

Mt 26:62-68 "And the high priest arose, and said unto him, Answerest thou nothing? what *is it which* these witness against thee? But Jesus held his peace. And the high priest answered and said unto him, I adjure thee by the living God, that thou tell us whether thou be the Christ, the Son of God. Jesus saith unto him, Thou hast said: nevertheless I say unto you, Hereafter shall ye see the Son of man sitting on the right hand of power, and coming in the clouds of heaven. Then the high priest rent his clothes, saying, He hath spoken blasphemy; what further need have we of witnesses? behold, now ye have heard his blasphemy. What think ye? They answered and said, He is guilty of death. Then did they spit in his face, and buffeted him; and others smote *him* with the palms of their hands, Saying, Prophesy unto us, thou Christ, Who is he that smote thee?"

Mt 27:11-14 "And Jesus stood before the governor: and the governor asked him, saying, Art thou the King of the Jews? And Jesus said unto him, Thou sayest. And when he was accused of the chief priests and elders, he answered nothing. Then said Pilate unto him, Hearest thou not how many things they witness against thee? And he answered him to never a word; insomuch that the governor marvelled greatly."

Lu 23:6-11 "When Pilate heard of Galilee, he asked whether the man were a Galilaean. And as soon as he knew that he belonged unto Herod's jurisdiction, he sent him to Herod, who himself also was at Jerusalem at that time. And when Herod saw Jesus, he was exceeding glad: for he was desirous to see him of a long *season*, because he had heard many things of him; and he hoped to have seen some miracle done by him. Then he questioned with him in many words; but he answered him nothing. And the chief priests and scribes stood and vehemently accused him. And Herod with his men of war set him at nought, and mocked *him*, and arrayed him in a gorgeous robe, and sent him again to Pilate."

Mt 27:22-26 "Pilate saith unto them, What shall I do then with Jesus which is called Christ? *They* all say unto him, Let him be crucified. And the governor said, Why, what evil hath he done? But they cried out the more, saying, Let him be crucified. When Pilate saw that he could prevail nothing, but *that* rather a tumult was made, he took water, and washed *his* hands before the multitude, saying, I am innocent of the blood of this just person: see ye *to it*. Then answered all the people, and said, His blood *be* on us, and on our children. Then released he Barabbas unto them: and when he had scourged Jesus, he delivered *him* to be crucified."

Christ's Suffering On the Cross:

Jesus suffered all the agonies of Calvary for the sake of souls:

2Co 5:21 "For he hath made him *to be* sin for us, who knew no sin; that we might be made the righteousness of God in him."

Mt 27:45-46 "Now from the sixth hour there was darkness over all the land unto the ninth hour. And about the ninth hour Jesus cried with a loud voice, saying, Eli, Eli, lama sabachthani? that is to say, My God, my God, why hast thou forsaken me?"

Joh 19:28-30 "After this, Jesus knowing that all things were now accomplished, that the scripture might be fulfilled, saith, I thirst. Now there was set a vessel full of vinegar: and they filled a spunge with vinegar, and put *it* upon hyssop, and put *it* to his mouth. When Jesus therefore had received the vinegar, he said, It is finished: and he bowed his head, and gave up the ghost."

The Worth of a Soul Must Be Measured by the Torments of Hell:

Every Person who Dies Without Christ will Spend Eternity in Hell:

Re 20:15 "And whosoever was not found written in the book of life was cast into the lake of fire."

Re 21:8 "But the fearful, and unbelieving, and the abominable, and murderers, and whoremongers, and sorcerers, and idolaters, and all liars, shall have their part in the lake which burneth with fire and brimstone: which is the second death."

Hell is a Place of Flames:

Jesus warned of the awful fire of hell:

Mt 18:8-9 "Wherefore if thy hand or thy foot offend thee, cut them off, and cast *them* from thee: it is better for thee to enter into life halt or maimed, rather than having two hands or two feet to be cast into everlasting fire. And if thine eye offend thee, pluck it out, and cast *it* from thee: it is better for thee to enter into life with one eye, rather than having two eyes to be cast into hell fire."

Hell is the place where the unsaved will spend eternity:

Re 14:11 "And the smoke of their torment ascendeth up for ever and ever: and they have no rest day nor night..."

Re 20:10 "And the devil that deceived them was cast into the lake of fire and brimstone, where the beast and the false prophet *are*, and shall be tormented day and night for ever and ever."

Hell is a Place of Conscious Suffering:

Lu 16:19-25 "There was a certain rich man, which was clothed in purple and fine linen, and fared sumptuously every day: And there was a certain beggar named Lazarus, which was laid at his gate, full of sores, And desiring to be fed with the crumbs which fell from the rich man's table: moreover the dogs came and licked his sores. And it came to pass, that the beggar died, and was carried by the angels into Abraham's bosom: the rich man also died, and was buried; And in hell he lift up his eyes, being in torments, and seeth Abraham afar off, and Lazarus in his bosom. And he cried and said, Father Abraham, have mercy on me, and send Lazarus, that he may dip the tip of his finger in water, and cool my tongue; for I am tormented in this flame. But Abraham said, Son, remember that thou in thy lifetime receivedst thy good things, and likewise Lazarus evil things: but now he is comforted, and thou art tormented."

This rich man who went to hell was tormented; he was thirsty; he remembered. He was as conscious in hell as he was upon the earth.

Hell is a Place of Eternal Suffering:

Hell is a place of no escape; no relief; no hope.

The Worth of a Soul Must Be Measured by the Glories of Heaven:

What is Heaven Like?

Heaven is a place of in incomparable beauty.

Heaven is a place of unending bliss.

Heaven is a place of uninterrupted peace.

Heaven is a place of glorious freedom- freedom from sin, death, fear, pain, sorrow, tears, weariness, weakness, and darkness.

Heaven is a place of unlimited enjoyment of God.

Heaven is a place of unprecedented fellowship with others.

Re 21:2-4 "And I John saw the holy city, new Jerusalem, coming down from God out of heaven, prepared as a bride adorned for her husband. And I heard a great voice out of heaven saying, Behold, the tabernacle of God *is* with men, and he will dwell with them, and they shall be his people, and God himself shall be with them, *and be* their God. And God shall wipe away all tears from their eyes; and there shall be no more death, neither sorrow, nor crying, neither shall there be any more pain: for the former things are passed away."

Joh 14:1-3 "Let not your heart be troubled: ye believe in God, believe also in me. In my Father's house are many mansions: if *it were* not *so,* I would have told you. I go to prepare a place for you. And if I go and prepare a place for you, I will come again, and receive you unto myself; that where I am, *there* ye may be also."

The Worth of a Soul Must Be Measured by the Love of God:

The Love of God is Measureless:

Henry Moorehouse began preaching at the age of sixteen. He died in early manhood. Every time he stood to preach, he gave as his text John 3:16:

Joh 3:16 "For God so loved the world, that he gave his only begotten Son, that whosoever believeth in him should not perish, but have everlasting life."

Why? Because God's love is immeasurable and inexhaustible.

The Worth of a Soul is Likewise Immeasurable:

Your soul is your most valuable possession, and the souls of others are of equal value. What are we doing to show our appreciation for the worth of souls?

The great evangelist, George Whitfield prayed, "Oh, God, give me souls, or take my soul!"

John Hyde prayed for India and said, "God, give me these souls, or I die!"

Have you assured the salvation of your own soul by believing on the Lord Jesus Christ? As a Christian, are you seeking the salvation of the souls of others through prayer and soul-winning? God the Father sent His Son, Jesus Christ, to save our souls. He gave His all for us. What will we give for Him?

"I Gave My Life for Thee"

I gave My life for thee,

My precious blood I shed,

That thou might ransomed be,

And quickened from the dead;

I gave, I gave My life for thee,

What hast thou giv'n for Me?

I gave, I gave My life for thee,

What hast thou giv'n for Me?

My Father's house of light,

My glory-circled throne

I left for earthly night,

For wand'rings sad and lone;

I left, I left it all for thee,

Hast thou left aught for Me?

I left, I left it all for thee,

Hast thou left aught for Me?

I suffered much for thee,

More than thy tongue can tell,

Of bitt'rest agony,

To rescue thee from hell;

I've borne, I've borne it all for thee,

What hast thou borne for Me?

I've borne, I've borne it all for thee,

What hast thou borne for Me?

And I have brought to thee,

Down from My home above,

Salvation full and free,

My pardon and My love;

I bring, I bring rich gifts to thee,

What hast thou brought to Me?

I bring, I bring rich gifts to thee,

What hast thou brought to Me?

-Frances R. Havergal, 1858

Chapter 4

The Wondrous Gift of Salvation
(Preached on January 6, 2000)

1Pe 1:10-12 "Of which salvation the prophets have inquired and searched diligently, who prophesied of the grace *that should come* unto you: Searching what, or what manner of time the Spirit of Christ which was in them did signify, when it testified beforehand the sufferings of Christ, and the glory that should follow. Unto whom it was revealed, that not unto themselves, but unto us they did minister the things, which are now reported unto you by them that have preached the gospel unto you with the Holy Ghost sent down from heaven; which things the angels desire to look into."

The theme of these verses is the salvation which may be found by faith in Jesus Christ. In writing about this salvation, the Apostle Peter reveals three things concerning this wondrous gift of God: The Prophets penned it; the Apostles proclaimed it; and the Angels ponder it.

<u>The Prophets Penned It:</u>

1Pe 1:10-11 "Of which salvation the prophets have inquired and searched diligently, who prophesied of the grace *that should come* unto you: Searching what, or what manner of time the Spirit of Christ which was in them did signify, when it testified beforehand the sufferings of Christ, and the glory that should follow."

The Prophets Wrote the Scriptures through the Inspiration of the Holy Spirit of God:

2Pe 1:21 "For the prophecy came not in old time by the will of man: but holy men of God spake *as they were* moved by the Holy Ghost."

The Spirit of Christ was "in them."

The Old Testament Prophets Wrote About Christ:

They Wrote about His suffering and death:

Ge 3:15 "And I will put enmity between thee and the woman, and between thy seed and her seed; it shall bruise thy head, and thou shalt bruise his heel."

Ps 22:6-8, 13-18 "But I *am* a worm, and no man; a reproach of men, and despised of the people. All they that see me laugh me to scorn: they shoot out the lip, they shake the head, *saying*, He trusted on the LORD *that* he would deliver him: let him deliver him, seeing he delighted in him...They gaped upon me *with* their mouths, *as* a ravening and a roaring lion. I am poured out like water, and all my bones are out of joint: my heart is like wax; it is melted in the midst of my bowels. My strength is dried up like a potsherd; and my tongue cleaveth to my jaws; and thou hast brought me into the dust of death. For dogs have compassed me: the assembly of the wicked have inclosed me: they pierced my hands and my feet. I may tell all my bones: they look *and* stare upon me. They part my garments among them, and cast lots upon my vesture."

Isa 53:3-6 "He is despised and rejected of men; a man of sorrows, and acquainted with grief: and we hid as it were *our* faces from him; he was despised, and we esteemed him not. Surely he hath borne our griefs, and carried our sorrows: yet we did esteem him stricken, smitten of God, and afflicted. But he *was* wounded for our transgressions, *he was* bruised for our iniquities: the chastisement of our peace *was* upon him; and with his stripes we are healed. All we like sheep have gone astray; we have turned every one to his own way; and the LORD hath laid on him the iniquity of us all."

They Wrote of His Resurrection:

Ps 16:8-11 "I have set the LORD always before me: because *he is* at my right hand, I shall not be moved. Therefore my heart is glad, and my glory rejoiceth: my flesh also shall rest in hope. For thou wilt not leave my soul in hell; neither wilt thou suffer thine Holy One to see corruption. Thou wilt shew me the path of life: in thy presence *is* fulness of joy; at thy right hand *there are* pleasures for evermore."

Ac 2:23-32 "Him, being delivered by the determinate counsel and foreknowledge of God, ye have taken, and by wicked hands have crucified and slain: Whom God hath raised up, having loosed the pains of death: because it was not possible that he should be holden of it. For David speaketh concerning him, I foresaw the Lord always before my face, for he is on my right hand, that I should not be moved: Therefore did my heart rejoice, and my tongue was glad; moreover also my flesh shall rest in hope: Because thou wilt not leave my soul in hell, neither wilt thou suffer thine Holy One to see corruption. Thou hast made known to me the ways of life; thou shalt make me full of joy with thy countenance. Men *and* brethren, let me freely speak unto you of the patriarch David, that he is both dead and buried, and his sepulchre is with us unto this day. Therefore being a prophet, and knowing that God had sworn with an oath to him, that of the fruit of his loins, according to the flesh, he would raise up Christ to sit on his throne; He seeing this before spake of the resurrection of Christ, that his soul was not left in hell, neither his flesh did see corruption. This Jesus hath God raised up, whereof we all are witnesses."

They Wrote of Salvation By Grace:

Jer 31:31-34 "Behold, the days come, saith the LORD, that I will make a new covenant with the house of Israel, and with the house of Judah: Not according to the covenant that I made with their fathers in the day *that* I took them by the hand to bring them out of the land of Egypt; which my covenant they brake, although I was an husband unto them, saith the LORD: But this *shall be* the covenant that I will make with the house of Israel; After those days, saith the LORD, I will put my law in their inward parts, and write it in their hearts; and will be their God, and they shall be my people. And they shall teach no more every man his neighbour, and every man his brother, saying, Know the LORD: for they shall all know me, from the least of them unto the greatest of them, saith the LORD: for I will forgive their iniquity, and I will remember their sin no more."

Heb 8:7-13 "For if that first *covenant* had been faultless, then should no place have been sought for the second. For finding fault with them, he saith, Behold, the days come, saith the Lord, when I will make a new covenant with the house of Israel and with the house of Judah: Not according to the covenant that I made with their fathers in the day when I took them by the hand to lead them out of the land of Egypt; because they continued not in my covenant, and I regarded them not, saith the Lord. For this *is* the covenant that I will make with the house of Israel after those days, saith the Lord; I will put my laws into their mind, and write them in their hearts: and I will be to them a God, and they shall be to me a people: And they shall not teach every man his neighbour, and every man his brother, saying, Know the Lord: for all shall know me, from the least to the greatest. For I will be merciful to their unrighteousness, and their sins and their iniquities will I remember no more. In that he saith, A new *covenant*, he hath made the first old. Now that which decayeth and waxeth old *is* ready to vanish away."

The Prophets Pondered What They Wrote:

The Old Testament Prophets "Inquired" about what they wrote:

They longed to know more about the things God moved them to write about. They sought to understand it. They didn't fully understand what they were inspired to write- especially when it came to the sufferings of Christ and the glory that would follow. They could not fully enter into the truths concerning Christ's death, and resurrection, and exaltation in glory.

How blessed we are today to have the full revelation of God. These great prophets of God such as Moses, Isaiah, Joel, Amos, and many others had only a portion of God's revealed truth. We have it all today. How blessed we are to have "the rest of the story." Such privilege begets responsibility. We have a responsibility to **receive** the truth. We have a responsibility **to submit to** the truth. And we have a responsibility **to share** the truth.

They Searched Diligently"

These men of God earnestly sought to fully understand God's inspired Word, and they received insight by their diligent search:

1Pe 1:12 "Unto whom it was revealed, that not unto themselves, but unto us they did minister the things..."

God showed them that He was speaking of a Person and of events yet to come. He showed them that by their faithfulness they were serving future generations. They were laying the foundation for the Apostles and for all of us today.

The Apostles built on that foundation.

The Apostles Proclaimed It:

1 Pe 1:12 "...Unto whom it was revealed, that not unto themselves, but unto us they did minister the things, which are now reported unto you by them that have preached the gospel unto you with the Holy Ghost sent down from heaven..."

They Proclaimed Christ Crucified:

This was the message of Peter:

Ac 2:22-23 "Ye men of Israel, hear these words; Jesus of Nazareth, a man approved of God among you by miracles and wonders and signs, which God did by him in the midst of you, as ye yourselves also know: Him, being delivered by the determinate counsel and foreknowledge of God, ye have taken, and by wicked hands have crucified and slain:"

It was the message of Paul:

1Co 2:1-2 "And I, brethren, when I came to you, came not with excellency of speech or of wisdom, declaring unto you the testimony of God. For I determined not to know any thing among you, save Jesus Christ, and him crucified."

It is the only message that saves sinners:

Ro 1:16 "For I am not ashamed of the gospel of Christ: for it is the power of God unto salvation to every one that believeth; to the Jew first, and also to the Greek."

1Co 1:21-24 "For after that in the wisdom of God the world by wisdom knew not God, it pleased God by the foolishness of preaching to save them that believe. For the Jews require a sign, and the Greeks seek after wisdom: But we preach Christ crucified, unto the Jews a stumblingblock, and unto the Greeks foolishness; But unto them which are called, both Jews and Greeks, Christ the power of God, and the wisdom of God."

They Proclaimed the Resurrection of Christ:

It was Peter's message:

Ac 2:24 "Whom God hath raised up, having loosed the pains of death: because it was not possible that he should be holden of it."

It was Paul's message:

1Co 15:3-4 "For I delivered unto you first of all that which I also received, how that Christ died for our sins according to the scriptures; And that he was buried, and that he rose again the third day according to the scriptures:"

It must be our message today:

1Co 15:15-23 "Yea, and we are found false witnesses of God; because we have testified of God that he raised up Christ: whom he raised not up, if so be that the dead rise not. For if the dead rise not, then is not Christ raised: And if Christ be not raised, your faith _is_ vain; ye are yet in your sins. Then they also which are fallen asleep in Christ are perished. If in this life only we have hope in Christ, we are of all men most miserable. But now is Christ risen from the dead, _and_ become the firstfruits of them that slept. For since by man _came_ death, by man _came_ also the resurrection of the dead. For as in Adam all die, even so in Christ shall all be made alive. But every man in his own order: Christ the firstfruits; afterward they that are Christ's at his coming."

Christ's resurrection guarantees the resurrection of all who are saved by faith in Him.

They Proclaimed Christ's Imminent Return:

In the writings of both Paul and Peter, as well as in the Gospels, we read of the blessed truth that Jesus Christ is coming again. Thousands of Scriptures throughout the Bible speak of the return of Jesus Christ, and Christ Himself promised it:

Joh 14:3 "And if I go and prepare a place for you, I will come again, and receive you unto myself; that where I am, *there* ye may be also."

Jesus Christ is coming again to judge the world in righteousness (Ps. 9:8; Acts 16:31); but He will first come in the air for His own, and His coming could be at any moment:

1Co 15:51 -58 "Behold, I shew you a mystery; We shall not all sleep, but we shall all be changed, In a moment, in the twinkling of an eye, at the last trump: for the trumpet shall sound, and the dead shall be raised incorruptible, and we shall be changed. For this corruptible must put on incorruption, and this mortal *must* put on immortality. So when this corruptible shall have put on incorruption, and this mortal shall have put on immortality, then shall be brought to pass the saying that is written, Death is swallowed up in victory. O death, where *is* thy sting? O grave, where *is* thy victory? The sting of death *is* sin; and the strength of sin *is* the law. But thanks *be* to God, which giveth us the victory through our Lord Jesus Christ. Therefore, my beloved brethren, be ye stedfast, unmoveable, always abounding in the work of the Lord, forasmuch as ye know that your labour is not in vain in the Lord."

Jesus Christ was crucified in weakness, but He rose again in power. One day He is coming back in glory. Hallelujah!

The Angels Ponder It:

1Pe 1:12 "...which things the angels desire to look into."

The Angels are Interested in the Gospel:

The holy angels of God do not fully understand the Gospel. They cannot understand it by experience as redeemed sinners do. They have never known sin or its consequences first hand. They have observed it. They were witnesses of the fall of Satan and the fall of man.

The Angels are Participants in God's Redemptive Work

The angels announced Jesus' birth (Mt. 1:20-21; Lu.1:26-35; 2:8-15).

They ministered to Christ when He was upon the earth during His temptation and in the Garden of Gethsemane just prior to His crucifixion (Mt. 4:11; Mr. 1:13; Lu. 22:43).

The angels announced Christ's resurrection (Mt. 28:1-6).

The angels are involved in the warfare against Satan (Da. 10:12-13; Re. 12:7-9).

The angels will be very active during the Tribulation time as agents of God's judgment.

The Angels Have Never Experienced God's Grace:

The angels cannot fully comprehend the mercy and forgiveness of God through the new birth; therefore, they have an intense desire to understand the Gospel. They long to look into these things, and they are committed to the work and will of God. Angels have a special ministry and a close relationship to man, especially to the saved:

Heb 1:13-14 "But to which of the angels said he at any time, Sit on my right hand, until I make thine enemies thy footstool? Are they not all ministering spirits, sent forth to minister for them who shall be heirs of salvation?"

Oh, how wondrous is God's gift of salvation! The prophets penned it. The Apostles preached it. The angels ponder it. Now, what are we doing about it? What are we doing to spread this wondrous Gospel that has been entrusted to us by God's mercy and grace?

2Co 5:19-20 "To wit, that God was in Christ, reconciling the world unto himself, not imputing their trespasses unto them; and hath committed unto us the word of reconciliation. Now then we are ambassadors for Christ, as though God did beseech *you* by us: we pray *you* in Christ's stead, be ye reconciled to God."

God help us to go forth as His ambassadors to tell the wonderful story of Jesus and His love!

"Tell Me the Story of Jesus"

Tell me the story of Jesus,

Write on my heart every word;

Tell me the story most precious,

Sweetest that ever was heard.

Tell how the angels in chorus,

Sang as they welcomed His birth,

"Glory to God in the highest!

Peace and good tidings to earth."

Refrain:

Tell me the story of Jesus,

Write on my heart every word;

Tell me the story most precious,

Sweetest that ever was heard.

Fasting alone in the desert,

Tell of the days that are past,

How for our sins He was tempted,

Yet was triumphant at last.

Tell of the years of His labor,

Tell of the sorrow He bore;

He was despised and afflicted,

Homeless, rejected and poor.

Tell of the cross where they nailed Him,

Writhing in anguish and pain;

Tell of the grave where they laid Him,

Tell how He liveth again.

Love in that story so tender,

Clearer than ever I see;

Stay, let me weep while you whisper,

"Love paid the ransom for me."

Tell how He's gone back to heaven,

Up to the right hand of God:

How He is there interceding

While on this earth we must trod.

Tell of the sweet Holy Spirit

He has poured out from above;

Tell how He's coming in glory

For all the saints of His love.

Refrain:

Tell me the story of Jesus,

Write on my heart every word;

Tell me the story most precious,

Sweetest that ever was heard.

-Frances J. Crosby, 1880

Chapter 5

"Building For Eternity"
(Preached on June 6, 1975, at Victory Baptist Church, Chicago, Illinois)

1Co 3:11-15 "For other foundation can no man lay than that is laid, which is Jesus Christ. Now if any man build upon this foundation gold, silver, precious stones, wood, hay, stubble; Every man's work shall be made manifest: for the day shall declare it, because it shall be revealed by fire; and the fire shall try every man's work of what sort it is. If any man's work abide which he hath built thereupon, he shall receive a reward. If any man's work shall be burned, he shall suffer loss: but he himself shall be saved; yet so as by fire."

It is both a wonderful and a terrible thought to realize that all that we do in this life will in some sense affect our eternal state. It is wonderful in that we may increase our enjoyment and reward. It is terrible in that one may lose his reward or even increase his torment in the eternal flames of Hell. Today, I want us to consider the thought of "Building for Eternity." In this passage, the Apostle Paul portrays our life's work as a building which must endure the testing of God.

We Must Build on the Right Foundation- the Only Foundation: Jesus Christ

God Laid the Foundation:

Through Christ's suffering and death:

Ro 5:8 "But God commendeth his love toward us, in that, while we were yet sinners, Christ died for us."

2Co 5:21 "For he hath made him *to be* sin for us, who knew no sin; that we might be made the righteousness of God in him."

Isa 53:5-6 "But he *was* wounded for our transgressions, *he was* bruised for our iniquities: the chastisement of our peace *was* upon him; and with his stripes we are healed. All we like sheep have gone astray; we have turned every one to his own way; and the LORD hath laid on him the iniquity of us all."

Through Christ's Resurrection and Ascension into Glory:

Ro 4:24-25 "But for us also, to whom it shall be imputed, if we believe on him that raised up Jesus our Lord from the dead; Who was delivered for our offences, and was raised again for our justification."

Jesus' resurrection demonstrated God's acceptance of His sacrifice on the cross:

Isa 53:11 'He shall see of the travail of his soul, *and* shall be satisfied: by his knowledge shall my righteous servant justify many; for he shall bear their iniquities."

Christ's resurrection demonstrated His power over Satan, sin, and death:

Through Christ's Intercession for Us:

Jesus Christ is our eternal Intercessor:

Heb 7:25 "Wherefore he is able also to save them to the uttermost that come unto God by him, seeing he ever liveth to make intercession for them."

Through Christ's Indwelling Presence:

Ga 2:20 "I am crucified with Christ: nevertheless I live; yet not I, but Christ liveth in me: and the life which I now live in the flesh I live by the faith of the Son of God, who loved me, and gave himself for me."

The Foundation is Christ and Salvation by Grace through Faith in Him:

Faith Receives what God has Already Provided in Christ:

Salvation is God's Work of Grace:

Eph 2:8-9 "For by grace are ye saved through faith; and that not of yourselves: *it is* the gift of God: Not of works, lest any man should boast."

Faith in Christ Receives a Completed Salvation:

Every saved person is justified, reconciled, forgiven, and sanctified:

Ro 8:30 "Moreover whom he did predestinate, them he also called: and whom he called, them he also justified: and whom he justified, them he also glorified."

1Co 1:30-31 "But of him are ye in Christ Jesus, who of God is made unto us wisdom, and righteousness, and sanctification, and redemption: That, according as it is written, He that glorieth, let him glory in the Lord."

Eternal Life is a Gift of God:

Salvation can never be earned. Good works have nothing to do with God's acceptance of us. We are sinners and could never be accepted on our merit. We are accepted by God on the ground of our perfect Savior and His sacrifice in our place.

Good works are the fruit of salvation and have to do with rewards. Our works have to do with building on the foundation already laid- Jesus Christ.

Jesus Illustrated this Truth in the Parable of the Wise and Foolish Builders:

Mt 7:24-29 "Therefore whosoever heareth these sayings of mine, and doeth them, I will liken him unto a wise man, which built his house upon a rock: And the rain descended, and the floods came, and the winds blew, and beat upon that house; and it fell not: for it was founded upon a rock. And every one that heareth these sayings of mine, and doeth them not, shall be likened unto a foolish man, which built his house upon the sand: And the rain descended, and the floods came, and the winds blew, and beat upon that house; and it fell: and great was the fall of it. And it came to pass, when Jesus had ended these sayings, the people were astonished at his doctrine: For he taught them as *one* having authority, and not as the scribes."

This parable illustrates two ways to build a life. The only difference was the foundation upon which they built:

Sand represents the many alternatives to true salvation that Satan offers. It represents self-effort and self-righteousness. Human works and religion are not the foundation of a life acceptable to God. No building will pass the test of God's righteousness unless it is built upon Jesus' blood and His righteousness.

The house built upon the rock represents the life built upon Jesus Christ and His Word. For the Christian, all works done outside of Christ's strength are wood, hay, and stubble. Only God working in us enables us to do works pleasing to Him:

Heb 13:20-21 "Now the God of peace, that brought again from the dead our Lord Jesus, that great shepherd of the sheep, through the blood of the everlasting covenant, Make you perfect in every good work to do his will, working in you that which is wellpleasing in his sight, through Jesus Christ; to whom *be* glory for ever and ever. Amen."

Php 2:12-13 "Wherefore, my beloved, as ye have always obeyed, not as in my presence only, but now much more in my absence, work out your own salvation with fear and trembling. For it is God which worketh in you both to will and to do of *his* good pleasure."

1Th 1:3 "Remembering without ceasing your work of faith, and labour of love, and patience of hope in our Lord Jesus Christ, in the sight of God and our Father;"

<u>Every Person's Works will be Tried:</u>

As To Motive:

1Co 4:5 "Therefore judge nothing before the time, until the Lord come, who both will bring to light the hidden things of darkness, and will make manifest the counsels of the hearts: and then shall every man have praise of God."

Only work done from a loving heart is acceptable unto God:

1Co 13:1-7 "Though I speak with the tongues of men and of angels, and have not charity, I am become *as* sounding brass, or a tinkling cymbal. And though I have *the gift of* prophecy, and understand all mysteries, and all knowledge; and though I have all faith, so that I could remove mountains, and have not charity, I am nothing. And though I bestow all my goods to feed *the poor*, and though I give my body to be burned, and have not charity, it profiteth me nothing. Charity suffereth long, *and* is kind; charity envieth not; charity vaunteth not itself, is not puffed up, Doth not behave itself unseemly, seeketh not her own, is not easily provoked, thinketh no evil; Rejoiceth not in iniquity, but rejoiceth in the truth; Beareth all things, believeth all things, hopeth all things, endureth all things."

Only works done for the glory of God will be acceptable to Him:

Why we do things is just as important as what we do. It is possible to give, to go, to do- but all for selfish motives. Pride, ambition, self-glory, and the fear of man are not right motives. This is why we must seek God and His power and abide in Christ that His glory may flow through our lives in service to Him.

As to Right or Wrong:

2Co 5:10 "For we must all appear before the judgment seat of Christ; that every one may receive the things *done* in *his* body, according to that he hath done, whether *it be* good or bad."

How do we know what is good or bad? We find the truth of what is right and wrong in the Word of God and through the example of Jesus Christ.

As to Faithfulness:

We see a clear picture of faithfulness in the parable of the talents in Matthew 25:

Mt 25:14-30 "For *the kingdom of heaven is* as a man travelling into a far country, *who* called his own servants, and delivered unto them his goods. And unto one he gave five talents, to another two, and to another one; to every man according to his several ability; and straightway took his journey. Then he that had received the five talents went and traded with the same, and made *them* other five talents. And likewise he that *had received* two, he also gained other two. But he that had received one went and digged in the earth, and hid his lord's money. After a long time the lord of those servants cometh, and reckoneth with them. And so he that had received five talents came and brought other five talents, saying, Lord, thou deliveredst unto me five talents: behold, I have gained beside them five talents more. His lord said unto him, Well done, *thou* good and faithful servant: thou hast been faithful over a few things, I will make thee ruler over many things: enter thou into the joy of thy lord. He also that had received two talents came and said, Lord, thou deliveredst unto me two talents: behold, I have gained two other talents beside them. His lord said unto him, Well done, good and faithful servant; thou hast been faithful over a few things, I will make thee ruler over many things: enter thou into the joy of thy lord. Then he which had received the one talent came and said, Lord, I knew thee that thou art an hard man, reaping where thou hast not sown, and gathering where thou hast not strawed: And I was afraid, and went and hid thy talent in the earth: lo, *there* thou hast *that is* thine. His lord answered and said unto him, *Thou* wicked and slothful servant, thou knewest that I reap where I sowed not, and gather where I have not strawed: Thou oughtest therefore to have put my money to the exchangers, and *then* at my coming I should have received mine own with usury. Take therefore the talent from him, and give *it* unto him which hath ten talents. For unto every one that hath shall be given, and he shall have abundance: but from him that hath not shall be taken away even that which he hath. And cast ye the unprofitable servant into outer darkness: there shall be weeping and gnashing of teeth."

The talents in this passage represent light and opportunity, abilities, and spiritual gifts given by God. Those who have greater privilege will have greater responsibility.

All Works Will be Tried by Fire:

1Co 3:13 "Every man's work shall be made manifest: for the day shall declare it, because it shall be revealed by fire; and the fire shall try every man's work of what sort it is."

The fire of God's presence and holiness will try every person's work "of what sort it is":

Heb 12:28-29 "Wherefore we receiving a kingdom which cannot be moved, let us have grace, whereby we may serve God acceptably with reverence and godly fear: For our God *is* a consuming fire."

Various Materials with which We May Build:

Three of these represent acceptable service:

Gold *represents spiritual service done in dependence upon God*

Silver *represents sacrificial service.*

Precious Stones *represent steadfast service.*

Three of these represent unacceptable service:

Wood *represents careless service*

Hay *represents costless service*

Stubble *represents worthless service.*

<u>**There Will Be Either Reward or Loss:**</u>

Our Works will Honor or Dishonor Christ.

Our Works will Bring Eternal Joy or Shame at the Judgment Seat of Christ:

1Jo 2:28 And now, little children, abide in him; that, when he shall appear, we may have confidence, and not be ashamed before him at his coming.

2Pe 1:10-11 "Wherefore the rather, brethren, give diligence to make your calling and election sure: for if ye do these things, ye shall never fall: For so an entrance shall be ministered unto you abundantly into the everlasting kingdom of our Lord and Saviour Jesus Christ."

To Live is Christ

There Will Be Shame and Loss for the Unfaithful Christian:

1Co 3:15 "If any man's work shall be burned, he shall suffer loss: but he himself shall be saved; yet so as by fire."

The unfaithful Christian will suffer the disapproval of God, of all the saints, and of the angels. There will be sadness and the stripping away of the reward which might have been received.

There Will Be Reward for the Faithful Christian:

1Co 3:14 "If any man's work abide which he hath built thereupon, he shall receive a reward."

There will be greater enjoyment and rejoicing in Christ's presence, and more treasures in Heaven for the faithful Christian.

Treasures Laid up In Heaven Include:

Money invested in Christ's service

Time invested in God's work

Souls saved through our influence

Prayers prayed for God's glory

Conclusion:

If you have not already, begin to build on the one foundation- Jesus Christ -by trusting Him for salvation. As a Christian, live your life in readiness and expectation for Jesus to come and walk in the power of the Holy Spirit each day that your life may be a precious offering to God at the Judgment Seat of Christ.

"The Solid Rock"

My hope is built on nothing less

Than Jesus' blood and righteousness;

I dare not trust the sweetest frame,

But wholly lean on Jesus' name.

Refrain:

On Christ, the solid Rock, I stand;

All other ground is sinking sand,

All other ground is sinking sand.

When darkness seems to hide His face,

I rest on His unchanging grace;

In every high and stormy gale,

My anchor holds within the veil.

His oath, His covenant, His blood

Support me in the whelming flood;

When all around my soul gives way,

He then is all my hope and stay.

Refrain:

On Christ, the solid Rock, I stand;

All other ground is sinking sand,

All other ground is sinking sand.

When He shall come with trumpet sound,

Oh, may I then in Him be found;

Dressed in His righteousness alone,

Faultless to stand before the throne.

Refrain:

On Christ, the solid Rock, I stand;

All other ground is sinking sand,

All other ground is sinking sand.

-Edward Mote, 1834

Chapter 6

"Stand Up and Be Counted"

(Preached on November 11, 1982, at First Baptist Church, Grayson, Kentucky)

Php 1:27-30 "Only let your conversation be as it becometh the gospel of Christ: that whether I come and see you, or else be absent, I may hear of your affairs, that ye stand fast in one spirit, with one mind striving together for the faith of the gospel; And in nothing terrified by your adversaries: which is to them an evident token of perdition, but to you of salvation, and that of God. For unto you it is given in the behalf of Christ, not only to believe on him, but also to suffer for his sake; Having the same conflict which ye saw in me, and now hear *to be* in me."

These verses we have read were written by the Apostle Paul from prison. Paul had been imprisoned for the preaching of the Gospel of Jesus Christ. In the verses just preceding, he had written of the great inward conflict which he was having- a desire to depart this life and be with Christ and a desire to remain that he might continue the great work God had given him to do among them -to strengthen them in the faith of Jesus Christ.

Paul was exhorting these believers in these verses that whether I am able to come and see you or not, I want you to amount to something for God. I want you to STAND UP AND BE COUNTED!

Too many Christians never amount to anything for God. Oh, how we need Christians who will stand up and be counted today- when it means being different; when it means sacrifice; when it means suffering; when it means work; when it means conflict; when it means praying; when it means self-denial; when it means witnessing; and when it means separation. Stand up, and be counted for Jesus Christ.

Consider what it means to stand up and be counted in a way that honors the Gospel of Jesus Christ:

Stand Up and Be Counted by our Adornment of the Gospel

Php 1:27 "Only let your conversation be as it becometh the gospel of Christ..."

The world needs to see Christ in us. As Christians, we need to demonstrate the power of the Gospel and be:

Adorned by Proper Conduct:

The term "conversation" means manner of life. It has reference to the fact that we are citizens of Heaven, and we are to live according to the dictates of our Heavenly Sovereign and King, Almighty God, and our Savior, Jesus Christ:

Ro 13:12-14 "The night is far spent, the day is at hand: let us therefore cast off the works of darkness, and let us put on the armour of light. Let us walk honestly, as in the day; not in rioting and drunkenness, not in chambering and wantonness, not in strife and envying. But put ye on the Lord Jesus Christ, and make not provision for the flesh, to *fulfil* the lusts *thereof.*"

Ga 5:16 "*This* I say then, Walk in the Spirit, and ye shall not fulfil the lust of the flesh."

Tit 2:11-13 "For the grace of God that bringeth salvation hath appeared to all men, Teaching us that, denying ungodliness and worldly lusts, we should live soberly, righteously, and godly, in this present world; Looking for that blessed hope, and the glorious appearing of the great God and our Saviour Jesus Christ;"

As Christians, we ought to be different. We ought to:

Reflect the Love of Christ:

Mt 5:14-16 "Ye are the light of the world. A city that is set on an hill cannot be hid. Neither do men light a candle, and put it under a bushel, but on a candlestick; and it giveth light unto all that are in the house. Let your light so shine before men, that they may see your good works, and glorify your Father which is in heaven."

Reject the Lusts of the Flesh:

Ga 5:19-21 "Now the works of the flesh are manifest, which are *these*; Adultery, fornication, uncleanness, lasciviousness, Idolatry, witchcraft, hatred, variance, emulations, wrath, strife, seditions, heresies, Envyings, murders, drunkenness, revellings, and such like: of the which I tell you before, as I have also told *you* in time past, that they which do such things shall not inherit the kingdom of God."

Renounce the Ways of the World:

1Jo 2:15-17 "Love not the world, neither the things *that are* in the world. If any man love the world, the love of the Father is not in him. For all that *is* in the world, the lust of the flesh, and the lust of the eyes, and the pride of life, is not of the Father, but is of the world. And the world passeth away, and the lust thereof: but he that doeth the will of God abideth for ever."

Reproduce the Fruit of the Spirit:

Ga 5:22-23 "But the fruit of the Spirit is love, joy, peace, longsuffering, gentleness, goodness, faith, Meekness, temperance: against such there is no law."

This is only possible through the power of the Holy Spirit. By yielding to His control, our lives ought to be supernatural lives through which we see:

-Prayers answered

-Souls won to Jesus Christ

-Victory over sin

-Joy in the midst of trials

Our lives are to be living epistles of Christ, read by all who are around us:

2Co 3:2-3 "Ye are our epistle written in our hearts, known and read of all men: *Forasmuch as ye are* manifestly declared to be the epistle of Christ ministered by us, written not with ink, but with the Spirit of the living God; not in tables of stone, but in fleshy tables of the heart."

Adorned by Courage:

Standing requires courage:

Php 1:28 "And in nothing terrified by your adversaries: which is to them an evident token of perdition, but to you of salvation, and that of God."

Standing Proves Something:

Standing for Christ and the Gospel proves that we are truly saved. It takes God's power to overcome fear, to stand in the face of persecution and temptation, to love, to forgive, and to deny self.

Standing Projects Something:

-The Damnation of the Unsaved- The stand of the Christian illuminates the fact that men apart from Christ are lost and will someday spend eternity in hell.

-The Defeat of Satan- Satan is a defeated foe, and when Christians stand fully adorned with the righteousness of Christ and the armor of God, we are taking the position given to us in Christ- as crucified with Him, risen with Him, and seated in Heavenly places in glory:

Eph 2:4-6 "But God, who is rich in mercy, for his great love wherewith he loved us, Even when we were dead in sins, hath quickened us together with Christ, (by grace ye are saved;) And hath raised _us_ up together, and made _us_ sit together in heavenly _places_ in Christ Jesus:"

As victorious Christians, yielded to Christ and His power, we reflect our Savior's final defeat of Satan, and the certain truth that the devil will one day be cast into the lake of fire forever.

Stand Up and Be Counted By our Accord in the Gospel:

Php 1:27b "...that whether I come and see you, or else be absent, I may hear of your affairs, that ye stand fast in one spirit, with one mind striving together for the faith of the gospel;"

The Greek word translated "striving together" is "sunathleo" and means "to wrestle in company with, i.e. (figuratively) to seek jointly:--labour with, strive together for" (Strong, G4866). As believers, nothing is more important than to be unified in this great struggle for the Gospel of Jesus Christ. On the day of Pentecost and following, the early church had this oneness of purpose and yieldedness to the Holy Spirit of God:

Ac 2:46-47 "And they, continuing daily with one accord in the temple, and breaking bread from house to house, did eat their meat with gladness and singleness of heart, Praising God, and having favour with all the people. And the Lord added to the church daily such as should be saved."

As believers, we have:

A Common Enemy- Satan

A Common Cause- To Spread the Gospel

A Common Commodity to Offer- Salvation in Jesus Christ and the truth of the Word of God

But if our unity is hindered by unconfessed sin- selfishness, pride, bad attitudes, lack of forgiveness, worldliness, lukewarmness, envy, lust, immorality, etc., we will fail in our mission.

Unity comes as we yield to the Holy Spirit of God. It comes as we are committed to obeying the Word of God. It is greatly influenced by the leadership of Spirit-filled pastors and godly leadership in the church.

We need accord in the following areas:

Accord in Our Commitment to the Gospel:

Php 1:27 "...striving together for the faith of the gospel;"

The "faith of the gospel" includes the whole body of truth included in the Scriptures- inspiration of the Bible, the deity of Christ, the virgin birth, etc.

Ac 20:26-28 "Wherefore I take you to record this day, that I *am* pure from the blood of all *men*. For I have not shunned to declare unto you all the counsel of God. Take heed therefore unto yourselves, and to all the flock, over the which the Holy Ghost hath made you overseers, to feed the church of God, which he hath purchased with his own blood."

Accord in Our Communication of the Gospel: Soul-Winning:

Nothing unifies us more than winning souls to Jesus Christ.

Standing Together in the Adversity of the Gospel:

Php 1:29-30 "For unto you it is given in the behalf of Christ, not only to believe on him, but also to suffer for his sake; Having the same conflict which ye saw in me, and now hear *to be* in me."

We Must Stand By Our Willingness to Pay the Cost:

For the Christian, this means self-denial. We must be willing to go the way of the cross and put the souls of others before our own interests. Sometimes, standing means loss, shame, reproach, and suffering. If we are going to stand, we must be different from the lost world.

We Must Stand By Willingness to Face Conflict:

As Christians, we are in a war. In this war, our enemies are the world, the flesh, and the devil:

1Jo 2:16-17 "For all that *is* in the world, the lust of the flesh, and the lust of the eyes, and the pride of life, is not of the Father, but is of the world. And the world passeth away, and the lust thereof: but he that doeth the will of God abideth for ever."

1Jo 4:4 "Ye are of God, little children, and have overcome them: because greater is he that is in you, than he that is in the world."

Ephesians 6:10-18 tells us how we can stand. We must stand by being strong in the Lord, and in the power of His might:

Eph 6:10-18 "Finally, my brethren, be strong in the Lord, and in the power of his might. Put on the whole armour of God, that ye may be able to stand against the wiles of the devil. For we wrestle not against flesh and blood, but against principalities, against powers, against the rulers of the darkness of this world, against spiritual wickedness in high *places*. Wherefore take unto you the whole armour of God, that ye may be able to withstand in the evil day, and having done all, to stand. Stand therefore, having your loins girt about with truth, and having on the breastplate of righteousness; And your feet shod with the preparation of the gospel of peace; Above all, taking the shield of faith, wherewith ye shall be able to quench all the fiery darts of the wicked. And take the helmet of salvation, and the sword of the Spirit, which is the word of God: Praying always with all prayer and supplication in the Spirit, and watching thereunto with all perseverance and supplication for all saints;"

Are you standing? Are you counting for God? Let us stand up and be counted!

"Stand Up, Stand Up For Jesus"

Stand up, stand up for Jesus! ye soldiers of the cross;

Lift high His royal banner, it must not suffer loss:

From vict'ry unto vict'ry, His army shall He lead,

Till every foe is vanquished, and Christ is Lord indeed.

Stand up, stand up for Jesus! The trumpet call obey:

Forth to the mighty conflict, in this His glorious day;

Ye that are men now serve Him against unnumbered foes;

Let courage rise with danger, and strength to strength oppose.

Stand up, stand up for Jesus! Stand in His strength alone,

The arm of flesh will fail you, ye dare not trust your own;

Put on the gospel armor, each piece put on with prayer,

Where duty calls or danger, be never wanting there.

Stand up, stand up for Jesus! the strife will not be long;

This day the noise of battle, the next the victor's song;

To him that overcometh a crown of life shall be;

He with the King of glory shall reign eternally.

-*George Duffield, Jr., 1858*

Chapter 7

"Dead Flies In the Ointment"
(Preached July 12, 1981, at Unity Baptist Church, Ashland, Kentucky)

Ec 10:1 "Dead flies cause the ointment of the apothecary to send forth a stinking savour: *so doth* a little folly him that is in reputation for wisdom *and* honour."

An apothecary is a druggist or pharmacist who mixed oils for different uses. Oils and ointments were used in many ways in both Old and New Testament times. There were four primary uses:

As a medicine

As a cosmetic perfume or lotion

As an ointment in burying the dead

As incense in religious ceremonies- both in heathen, idolatrous worship and in the true worship of Jehovah

As a holy anointing oil in the anointing of priests, prophets, and kings, as well as in the anointing of objects utilized in worship such as the tabernacle, the ark of the covenant, vessels, the altars, etc.

The formula for the anointing oil to be used in the worship of the LORD is given in Exodus 30:22-25:

Ex 30:22-25 "Moreover the LORD spake unto Moses, saying, Take thou also unto thee principal spices, of pure myrrh five hundred *shekels*, and of sweet cinnamon half so much, *even* two hundred and fifty *shekels*, and of sweet calamus two hundred and fifty *shekels*, And of cassia five hundred *shekels*, after the shekel of the sanctuary, and of oil olive an hin: And thou shalt make it an oil of holy ointment, an ointment compound after the art of the apothecary: it shall be an holy anointing oil."

This holy anointing oil is symbolic of the anointing power of God for service to Him:

Aaron and his sons were anointed to be the priests of the LORD.

Samuel, the prophet, anointed both Saul and David as kings of Israel.

Jesus is called the Christ, which means "the Anointed One" of God.

Oil is symbolic of the Holy Spirit throughout the Scriptures. So, in this picture of flies in the ointment, we note the following things:

The Condition of the Ointment:

This ointment mentioned was once useful and sweet smelling; but it is now foul-smelling and potentially harmful. The literal rendering of the term "dead flies" is "flies of death." The ointment has been fouled and made odious through neglect.

The Characterization of a Failed Testimony:

This picture of the despicable ointment fouled by death and decay may be symbolic of our own Christian testimony if marred by sin. Every Christian is sealed by the Holy Spirit, and is thus, set apart and consecrated to God as His own child. Every Christian is indwelt by the Holy Spirit of God and has the promise of power for service. We are commanded to be filled with the Holy Spirit (Eph. 5:18); but not every Christian is yielded to God for this enabling and filling work. The work of the Holy Spirit is to empower us for service and to enable us in prayer. Only He can produce the fruit of the Spirit in us:

Ga 5:22-23 "But the fruit of the Spirit is love, joy, peace, longsuffering, gentleness, goodness, faith, Meekness, temperance: against such there is no law."

The Picture in the Ointment:

The ointment filled with flies is a picture of an unyielded Christian- a Christian in whose life the Holy Spirit is grieved, hindered, and quenched. Sin is what hinders God's working and power in and through our lives. It is God's purpose to fill us with His Spirit, but any unyielded area or unconfessed sin constitutes a fly in the ointment.

The more flies there are and the longer they remain in the ointment, the more useless or potentially dangerous the ointment becomes. Sin mars our testimony and robs us of God's manifest presence in our lives. Only the Holy Spirit of God can produce the sweetness and healing power needed in our lives. It is God's purpose that every Christian should be fruitful and useful to Him; but sin hinders that purpose.

The Purpose of the Ointment:

The natural use of this ointment was for good:

To produce a sweet savor

To heal

To bring comfort or enjoyment

The Putrefying Effect:

The flies in the ointment made the oil repulsive and potentially deadly. Consider this in relationship to our Christian lives:

In relation to prayer:

No priest would burn incense in worship to holy God with a fly in it. In the same way, sin is a hindrance to our prayers:

Ps 66:18 "If I regard iniquity in my heart, the Lord will not hear *me:*"

In relation to our witness:

No priest would anoint another with a putrefied ointment- an ointment with flies in it. Sin takes away our power to win others to Christ or to help others grow in their relationship to Christ

To Live is Christ

In relation to our likeness to Christ:

No woman would put on such perfume- perfume with flies in it! In the same way, sin hinders our likeness to our lovely Savior and Lord.

In relation to our ministry to others:

What person would anoint a wound with oil full of dead, stinking flies? We cannot help to heal the gaping wounds of sin in the lives of others if our own lives are full of unconfessed sin.

In relation to the Holy Spirit's power and working through us:

The working of the Holy Ghost of God through our lives is marred by the dead flies of unconfessed and unforsaken sin.

The Cause of the Foul Condition of the Ointment:

It was **dead** flies which caused the ointment to stink. Every Christian sins:

1Jo 1:8 "If we say that we have no sin, we deceive ourselves, and the truth is not in us."

It is unconfessed sin which putrefies the life and spoils the oil of the Spirit of God working in our lives:

Sin breaks fellowship with God and with others.

Sin hinders our testimony before others.

Sin grieves the Holy Spirit and hinders His work through us.

It may be unrecognized sin in our lives that we need to see:

Under the Old Testament law, even sins of ignorance had to be atoned for.

A Christian may be ignorant of the Word.

Christians often rationalize their sin and set aside the truth of God.

The Word of God tells us that when we are willing to come clean with God and confess our sin, He will cleanse us from all unrighteousness;

1Jo 1:9 "If we confess our sins, he is faithful and just to forgive us *our* sins, and to cleanse us from all unrighteousness."

Are There Some of These Dead Flies of Unconfessed or Unforsaken Sin in Your Life?

To face up to our sin is not a pleasant experience. God must do His work, and we must do ours. God does the work of conviction and revelation in our lives; and we must be willing to confess and forsake sin and receive His forgiveness and renewed fullness in our lives. It is then that we can claim the victory and enjoy the fullness of God's power once again:

Ps 51:1-4, 7-10, 12-13. "Have mercy upon me, O God, according to thy lovingkindness: according unto the multitude of thy tender mercies blot out my transgressions. Wash me throughly from mine iniquity, and cleanse me from my sin. For I acknowledge my transgressions: and my sin *is* ever before me. Against thee, thee only, have I sinned, and done *this* evil in thy sight: that thou mightest be justified when thou speakest, *and* be clear when thou judgest...Purge me with hyssop, and I shall be clean: wash me, and I shall be whiter than snow. Make me to hear joy and gladness; *that* the bones *which* thou hast broken may rejoice. Hide thy face from my sins, and blot out all mine iniquities. Create in me a clean heart, O God; and renew a right spirit within me...Restore unto me the joy of thy salvation; and uphold me *with thy* free spirit. *Then* will I teach transgressors thy ways; and sinners shall be converted unto thee."

Some Examples of Dead Flies:

Pride- self dependence, bragging, haughtiness, lack of compassion, love of praise, unfriendliness, spiritual pride, stubbornness

Jealousy and Envy

Immorality- an evil eye, evil thoughts, indecent dress, sinful actions

Unclean habits- filling our minds with impure thoughts through what we watch, read, listen to, and dwell upon

Hypocrisy- living a phony spiritual life before God and others, but no true walk with God

Selfishness

Fear of Man

Indifference

Rebellion

Lack of Love

Unkindness- even within the family

Lack of forgiveness

Unbelief

Worry

Anger

Critical spirit

Laziness

Neglect

Disobedience

God has given us the power and the remedy for all of these things. Through confession and repentance we can clean the flies out of the ointment. We can be a sweet savor to God and to others again:

2Co 2:14-17 "Now thanks *be* unto God, which always causeth us to triumph in Christ, and maketh manifest the savour of his knowledge by us in every place. For we are unto God a sweet savour of Christ, in them that are saved, and in them that perish: To the one *we are* the savour of death unto death; and to the other the savour of life unto life. And who *is* sufficient for these things? For we are not as many, which corrupt the word of God: but as of sincerity, but as of God, in the sight of God speak we in Christ."

"Let Him Have His Way With Thee"

Would you live for Jesus, and be always pure and good?

Would you walk with Him within the narrow road?

Would you have Him bear your burden, carry all your load?

Let Him have His way with thee.

Refrain:

His pow'r can make you what you ought to be;

His blood can cleanse your heart and make you free;

His love can fill your soul, and you will see

'Twas best for Him to have His way with thee.

Would you have Him make you free, and follow at His call?

Would you know the peace that comes by giving all?

Would you have Him save you, so that you need never fall?

Let Him have His way with thee.

Would you in His kingdom find a place of constant rest?

Would you prove Him true in providential test?

Would you in His service labor always at your best?

Let Him have His way with thee.

Refrain:

His pow'r can make you what you ought to be;

His blood can cleanse your heart and make you free;

His love can fill your soul, and you will see

'Twas best for Him to have His way with thee.

-*Cyrus S. Nusbaum, 1898*

Chapter 8

"A Call to Prayer"
(Preached February 11, 1990)

Lu 18:1 -8 "And he spake a parable unto them *to this end*, that men ought always to pray, and not to faint; Saying, There was in a city a judge, which feared not God, neither regarded man: And there was a widow in that city; and she came unto him, saying, Avenge me of mine adversary. And he would not for a while: but afterward he said within himself, Though I fear not God, nor regard man; Yet because this widow troubleth me, I will avenge her, lest by her continual coming she weary me. And the Lord said, Hear what the unjust judge saith. And shall not God avenge his own elect, which cry day and night unto him, though he bear long with them? I tell you that he will avenge them speedily. Nevertheless when the Son of man cometh, shall he find faith on the earth?"

In this parable taught by Jesus Christ, we are given an encouragement to prayer. Now, if you are only slightly observant in the reading of this parable, you will find that there is only one point made, and that is the simple reality that God answers the prayers of His children. Thus, the thrust of this parable is simply this- that God answers prayer. That should be enough to call us to faithfulness in prayer. So, we have here an admonition that is a challenge to each one of us: "A Call to Prayer."

<u>It Is a Call to Faith in an Almighty God:</u>

God is a God who can and will answer prayer:

Jas 5:16-18 "Confess *your* faults one to another, and pray one for another, that ye may be healed. The effectual fervent prayer of a righteous man availeth much. Elias was a man subject to like passions as we are, and he prayed earnestly that it might not rain: and it rained not on the earth by the space of three years and six months. And he prayed again, and the heaven gave rain, and the earth brought forth her fruit."

Is God the God of the impossible?

Is He a God who keeps His promises?

Does God's power match our needs?

The answer to these questions is a resounding, "Yes!"

Eph 3:20-21 "Now unto him that is able to do exceeding abundantly above all that we ask or think, according to the power that worketh in us, Unto him *be* glory in the church by Christ Jesus throughout all ages, world without end. Amen."

The Bible Affirms the Fact that God Answers Prayer:

Mt 7:7-8 "Ask, and it shall be given you; seek, and ye shall find; knock, and it shall be opened unto you: For every one that asketh receiveth; and he that seeketh findeth; and to him that knocketh it shall be opened."

The Word of God Documents the Fact that God Answers Prayer:

This truth is shown throughout the Scriptures in the lives of God's people, both men and women. Consider the lives of Abraham, Moses, David, Nehemiah, and Hannah, just to name a few.

There Are Conditions for Answered Prayer:

-We must pray in faith, believing that God will answer:

Mr 11:24 Therefore I say unto you, What things soever ye desire, when ye pray, believe that ye receive *them*, and ye shall have *them*.

Jas 1:5-7 "If any of you lack wisdom, let him ask of God, that giveth to all *men* liberally, and upbraideth not; and it shall be given him. But let him ask in faith, nothing wavering. For he that wavereth is like a wave of the sea driven with the wind and tossed. For let not that man think that he shall receive any thing of the Lord."

-We must pray in the Spirit:

Eph 6:18 "Praying always with all prayer and supplication in the Spirit, and watching thereunto with all perseverance and supplication for all saints;"

-We must be living in obedience to God:

1Jo 3:21-22 "Beloved, if our heart condemn us not, *then* have we confidence toward God. And whatsoever we ask, we receive of him, because we keep his commandments, and do those things that are pleasing in his sight."

-We must pray in Jesus' name:

Joh 14:12-13 "Verily, verily, I say unto you, He that believeth on me, the works that I do shall he do also; and greater *works* than these shall he do; because I go unto my Father. And whatsoever ye shall ask in my name, that will I do, that the Father may be glorified in the Son."

-We must pray according to His will:

1Jo 5:14-15 "And this is the confidence that we have in him, that, if we ask any thing according to his will, he heareth us: And if we know that he hear us, whatsoever we ask, we know that we have the petitions that we desired of him."

-We must agree together in prayer:

Mt 18:19-20 "Again I say unto you, That if two of you shall agree on earth as touching any thing that they shall ask, it shall be done for them of my Father which is in heaven. For where two or three are gathered together in my name, there am I in the midst of them."

When God's conditions are met, God can and does answer prayer.

This Places the Burden upon the Believer:

To believe God

To meet God's conditions

To Live is Christ

To pray without ceasing (1Th. 5:17)

To believe God and pray for power, for victory, for souls, and for revival

*To believe God enough **to pray***

It is a Call to Habitual, Persistent, Urgent Prayer

Prayer Demands Discipline:

Christ was our example:

Mt 14:23 "And when he had sent the multitudes away, he went up into a mountain apart to pray: and when the evening was come, he was there alone."

Lu 6:12 "And it came to pass in those days, that he went out into a mountain to pray, and continued all night in prayer to God."

Lu 11:1 "And it came to pass, that, as he was praying in a certain place, when he ceased, one of his disciples said unto him, Lord, teach us to pray, as John also taught his disciples."

Prayer Demands Knowledge:

We need knowledge of God's Word to pray aright. We need knowledge of the needs of others so that we can pray for them.

Prayer Demands Commitment to God:

If we are not committed to God, we will not care or think to pray. We will be consumed with our own desires, not God's.

Prayer Demands a Walk of Fellowship in the Spirit:

It is the Spirit who helps our infirmities and intercedes for us in prayer according to the will of God:

Ro 8:26-27 "Likewise the Spirit also helpeth our infirmities: for we know not what we should pray for as we ought: but the Spirit itself maketh intercession for us with groanings which cannot be uttered. And he that searcheth the hearts knoweth what *is* the mind of the Spirit, because he maketh intercession for the saints according to *the will of* God."

Prayer Demands Persistence:

Lu 11:5-10 "And he said unto them, Which of you shall have a friend, and shall go unto him at midnight, and say unto him, Friend, lend me three loaves; For a friend of mine in his journey is come to me, and I have nothing to set before him? And he from within shall answer and say, Trouble me not: the door is now shut, and my children are with me in bed; I cannot rise and give thee. I say unto you, Though he will not rise and give him, because he is his friend, yet because of his importunity he will rise and give him as many as he needeth. And I say unto you, Ask, and it shall be given you; seek, and ye shall find; knock, and it shall be opened unto you. For every one that asketh receiveth; and he that seeketh findeth; and to him that knocketh it shall be opened."

Prayer Demands Urgency:

Jas 5:17 "Elias was a man subject to like passions as we are, and he prayed earnestly that it might not rain..."

Prayer Demands Faith:

Jas 1:6-7 "But let him ask in faith, nothing wavering. For he that wavereth is like a wave of the sea driven with the wind and tossed. For let not that man think that he shall receive any thing of the Lord."

Mt 17:20 "And Jesus said unto them, Because of your unbelief: for verily I say unto you, If ye have faith as a grain of mustard seed, ye shall say unto this mountain, Remove hence to yonder place; and it shall remove; and nothing shall be impossible unto you."

<u>It is a Call to Pray in All Circumstances and For Every Need</u>

Jesus encourages us to pray about everything:

To Live is Christ

We Should Pray for our Daily Needs:

Mt 6:11 "Give us this day our daily bread."

Prayer is dependence upon God. It demonstrates our dependence upon Him for everything.

We Should Pray for Strength and Grace:

Mt 6:12 "And forgive us our debts, as we forgive our debtors."

We Should Pray About our Problems and Troubles:

Mt 6:13 "And lead us not into temptation, but deliver us from evil..."

We Should Pray for Our Family Members

-For protection and grace'

-For spiritual enlightenment

-For godly companions

Paul's prayer for the Ephesian Christians is a wonderful example of how we should pray for others:

Eph 3:14-19 "For this cause I bow my knees unto the Father of our Lord Jesus Christ, Of whom the whole family in heaven and earth is named, That he would grant you, according to the riches of his glory, to be strengthened with might by his Spirit in the inner man; That Christ may dwell in your hearts by faith; that ye, being rooted and grounded in love, May be able to comprehend with all saints what *is* the breadth, and length, and depth, and height; And to know the love of Christ, which passeth knowledge, that ye might be filled with all the fulness of God."

We Should Pray First and Foremost for Spiritual Needs:

We are responsible to pray for "all saints":

Eph 6:18 "Praying always with all prayer and supplication in the Spirit, and watching thereunto with all perseverance and supplication for all saints;"

We are responsible to pray for lost souls:

1Ti 2:1-4 "I exhort therefore, that, first of all, supplications, prayers, intercessions, *and* giving of thanks, be made for all men; For kings, and *for* all that are in authority; that we may lead a quiet and peaceable life in all godliness and honesty. For this *is* good and acceptable in the sight of God our Saviour; Who will have all men to be saved, and to come unto the knowledge of the truth."

It is a Call Not to Faint

Lu 18:8 "...Nevertheless when the Son of man cometh, shall he find faith on the earth?"

There is a Grave Danger:

There is a danger- not that God will fail -but that His people will fail; and how does God's work go forward if not by prayer? In the light of God's most incredible promises, what is the most important work in the world? Is it not prayer- earnest, seeking prayer?

There is a Serious Lack of Faith:

How much of our praying is praying in faith? How much of our praying is prayer that continually cries out to God and believes God for the answer?

It is a Call to Every Believer

Every born again child of God has the privilege and responsibility to pray:

Heb 4:15-16 "For we have not an high priest which cannot be touched with the feeling of our infirmities; but was in all points tempted like as *we are, yet* without sin. Let us therefore come boldly unto the throne of grace, that we may obtain mercy, and find grace to help in time of need."

To Live is Christ

Any obedient Christian can be effective in prayer. Every Christian has the need to pray. All Christians are responsible to God to pray.

Will we accept the challenge?

"Did You Think To Pray"

Ere you left your room this morning,

Did you think to pray?

In the name of Christ our Savior,

Did you sue for loving favor,

As a shield today?

Refrain:

Oh, how praying rests the weary!

Prayer will change the night to day;

So when life seems dark and dreary,

Don't forget to pray.

When you met with great temptation,

Did you think to pray?

By His dying love and merit,

Did you claim the Holy Spirit

As your guide and stay?

When your heart was filled with anger,

Did you think to pray?

Did you plead for grace, my brother,

That you might forgive another

Who had crossed your way?

When sore trials came upon you,

Did you think to pray?

When your soul was bowed in sorrow,

Balm of Gilead did you borrow

At the gates of day?

Refrain:

Oh, how praying rests the weary!

Prayer will change the night to day;

So when life seems dark and dreary,

Don't forget to pray.

-*Mary A. Kidder, 1876*

Chapter 9

"The Harrows and Hosts of Hell"
(Preached April 22, 1991 at Stewart's Chapel Baptist Church)

Re 21:8 "But the fearful, and unbelieving, and the abominable, and murderers, and whoremongers, and sorcerers, and idolaters, and all liars, shall have their part in the lake which burneth with fire and brimstone: which is the second death."

Hell is a reality- a horrible reality. Listen, if Hell is not real, then there is no Heaven. If Hell is not real, then Jesus was a liar and a fake, because He declared it to be true. If there is no Hell, then the cross was the biggest mistake in history, Jesus Christ was a madman, and all of His followers are deluded fools. If Hell is a joke, then the evolutionists and infidels are right, the Bible is untrue, and Christianity is a farce. But Hell is real because Jesus Christ proved Himself to be real. Jesus and Hell stand or fall together. Since Jesus proved Himself to be the Son of God by His resurrection from the dead, there can be no question that He spoke the truth about all things- and He spoke the truth about Hell.

The Harrows of Hell

The Harrow of Unquenchable Fire:

Is there literal, burning fire in Hell? Jesus Christ said there is:

Mr 9:43-49 "And if thy hand offend thee, cut it off: it is better for thee to enter into life maimed, than having two hands to go into hell, into the **fire** that never shall be quenched: Where their worm dieth not, and the **fire** is not quenched. And if thy foot offend thee, cut it off: it is better for thee to enter halt into life, than having two feet to be cast into hell, into the **fire** that never shall be quenched: Where their worm dieth not, and the **fire** is not quenched. And if thine eye offend thee, pluck it out: it is better for thee to enter into the kingdom of God with one eye, than having two eyes to be cast into hell **fire**: Where their worm dieth not, and the **fire** is not quenched. For every one shall be salted with **fire**, and every sacrifice shall be salted with salt."

Seven times in this passage, Jesus used the word "fire." Five of those times, He spoke of fire that is not, or shall never be quenched. There is literal fire in Hell.

The Harrow of Unsatisfied Desires:

The harrow of unsatisfied desire is illustrated in the story Christ told of the rich man in hell who desired just a fingertip of water to cool his tongue in the flames of hell; but he could not have it:

Lu 16:23-24 "And in hell he lift up his eyes, being in torments, and seeth Abraham afar off, and Lazarus in his bosom. And he cried and said, Father Abraham, have mercy on me, and send Lazarus, that he may dip the tip of his finger in water, and cool my tongue; for I am tormented in this flame."

The Harrow of No Escape:

There is no exit from hell. It is a place of utter hopelessness and a place of no escape. Hopelessness is written upon every glowing ember, upon every leaping flame, and upon every anguished face in Hell. There is no hope of deliverance from that place.

The Harrow of Unspeakable Misery:

The rich man in Hell exclaimed, "I am tormented in this flame." Hell is a place of unspeakable torment- a place of pain, anguish, and unrest. There are no pain killers in Hell- no relief from its terrible torments.

The Hosts of Hell

We now turn to the inhabitants or "hosts" of Hell. In Hell, we find:

The Wicked:

Ps 9:17 "The wicked shall be turned into hell, *and* all the nations that forget God."

The wicked include the lawless and all transgressors of God's law:

1Jo 3:4 "Whosoever committeth sin transgresseth also the law: for sin is the transgression of the law."

1Co 6:9-10 "Know ye not that the unrighteous shall not inherit the kingdom of God? Be not deceived: neither fornicators, nor idolaters, nor adulterers, nor effeminate, nor abusers of themselves with mankind, Nor thieves, nor covetous, nor drunkards, nor revilers, nor extortioners, shall inherit the kingdom of God."

These verses are not saying that those guilty of these things cannot be saved; but that they must be saved to go to Heaven, as the next verse clearly teaches:

1Co 6:11 "And such **were** some of you: but ye are washed, but ye are sanctified, but ye are justified in the name of the Lord Jesus, and by the Spirit of our God."

The Fearful and Unbelieving:

Re 21:8 "But the fearful, and unbelieving, and the abominable, and murderers, and whoremongers, and sorcerers, and idolaters, and all liars, shall have their part in the lake which burneth with fire and brimstone: which is the second death."

Salvation in Christ alone is the only way anyone can be saved from the fires of Hell.

All Who Know Not God:

2Th 1:7-9 "And to you who are troubled rest with us, when the Lord Jesus shall be revealed from heaven with his mighty angels, In flaming fire taking vengeance on them that know not God, and that obey not the gospel of our Lord Jesus Christ: Who shall be punished with everlasting destruction from the presence of the Lord, and from the glory of his power;"

The story was told of a young lady who lay dying. As she lay upon the brink of death, she turned to her father who was present at the death bed and asked, "Father, why didn't you tell me there was a Hell? The father replied, "There is no such place!" The daughter cried, "I'm dying! And I know there is a Hell, for my feet are in the flames right now!" And she went out into eternity lost because she knew not God!

All Who Obey Not the Gospel of Our Lord Jesus Christ:

Hell is full of religionists, lost church members, and procrastinators who refused to accept the truth of the simple Gospel- by grace alone, through faith alone, in the work of Jesus Christ alone. This is the Gospel of our Lord Jesus Christ! So many refuse to obey this Gospel, and go their own way to eternal destruction:

Mt 7:13-14 "Enter ye in at the strait gate: for wide *is* the gate, and broad *is* the way, that leadeth to destruction, and many there be which go in thereat: Because strait *is* the gate, and narrow *is* the way, which leadeth unto life, and few there be that find it."

Joh 14:6 "Jesus saith unto him, I am the way, the truth, and the life: no man cometh unto the Father, but by me."

The Antichrist and all of his Followers:

Re 19:20 "And the beast was taken, and with him the false prophet that wrought miracles before him, with which he deceived them that had received the mark of the beast, and them that worshipped his image. These both were cast alive into a lake of fire burning with brimstone."

Satan and All of his Angels:

Re 20:10 "And the devil that deceived them was cast into the lake of fire and brimstone, where the beast and the false prophet *are*, and shall be tormented day and night for ever and ever."

All Whose Names are Not Written in the Book of Life:

Re 20:12-14 "And I saw the dead, small and great, stand before God; and the books were opened: and another book was opened, which is *the book* of life: and the dead were judged out of those things which were written in the books, according to their works. And the sea gave up the dead which were in it; and death and hell delivered up the dead which were in them: and they were judged every man according to their works. And death and hell were cast into the lake of fire. This is the second death."

The How of Not Going to Hell

God loves sinners like you and me. He does not want anyone to perish. He does not want you to go to Hell. God has made a way for you to escape the fires of Hell:

2Pe 3:9 "The Lord is not slack concerning his promise, as some men count slackness; but is longsuffering to us-ward, not willing that any should perish, but that all should come to repentance."

Believe the Truth of the Gospel:

Joh 3:16 For God so loved the world, that he gave his only begotten Son, that whosoever believeth in him should not perish, but have everlasting life.

Ro 5:8 "But God commendeth his love toward us, in that, while we were yet sinners, Christ died for us."

Get Your Sins Under the Blood:

Isa 53:5-6 "But he *was* wounded for our transgressions, *he was* bruised for our iniquities: the chastisement of our peace *was* upon him; and with his stripes we are healed. All we like sheep have gone astray; we have turned every one to his own way; and the LORD hath laid on him the iniquity of us all."

Receive Jesus Christ Into Your Life:

Ro 10:9-10 "That if thou shalt confess with thy mouth the Lord Jesus, and shalt believe in thine heart that God hath raised him from the dead, thou shalt be saved. For with the heart man believeth unto righteousness; and with the mouth confession is made unto salvation."

Don't Put Off Salvation:

2Co 6:2 "(For he saith, I have heard thee in a time accepted, and in the day of salvation have I succoured thee: behold, now *is* the accepted time; behold, now *is* the day of salvation.)"

Heb 2:3 "How shall we escape, if we neglect so great salvation; which at the first began to be spoken by the Lord, and was confirmed unto us by them that heard *him*;"

You don't have to go to Hell. Trust in Jesus Christ alone. Be saved today!

"Almost Persuaded"

"Almost persuaded" now to believe;

"Almost persuaded" Christ to receive;

Seems now some soul to say,

"Go, Spirit, go Thy way,

Some more convenient day

On Thee I'll call."

"Almost persuaded," come, come today;

"Almost persuaded," turn not away;

Jesus invites you here,

Angels are ling'ring near,

Prayers rise from hearts so dear;

O wand'rer, come!

"Almost persuaded," harvest is past!

"Almost persuaded," death comes at last!

"Almost" cannot avail;

"Almost" is but to fail!

Sad, sad, that bitter wail—

"Almost," but lost!

- Philip P. Bliss, pub.1871

Chapter 10

"Eternity's Insane Asylum"

(Preached September 2, 1990, at First Baptist Church, Grayson, Kentucky)

Re 20:11-15 "And I saw a great white throne, and him that sat on it, from whose face the earth and the heaven fled away; and there was found no place for them. And I saw the dead, small and great, stand before God; and the books were opened: and another book was opened, which is *the book* of life: and the dead were judged out of those things which were written in the books, according to their works. And the sea gave up the dead which were in it; and death and hell delivered up the dead which were in them: and they were judged every man according to their works. And death and hell were cast into the lake of fire. This is the second death. And whosoever was not found written in the book of life was cast into the lake of fire."

Re 21:1-8 "And I saw a new heaven and a new earth: for the first heaven and the first earth were passed away; and there was no more sea. And I John saw the holy city, new Jerusalem, coming down from God out of heaven, prepared as a bride adorned for her husband. And I heard a great voice out of heaven saying, Behold, the tabernacle of God *is* with men, and he will dwell with them, and they shall be his people, and God himself shall be with them, *and be* their God. And God shall wipe away all tears from their eyes; and there shall be no more death, neither sorrow, nor crying, neither shall there be any more pain: for the former things are passed away. And he that sat upon the throne said, Behold, I make all things new. And he said unto me, Write: for these words are true and faithful. And he said unto me, It is done. I am Alpha and Omega, the beginning and the end. I will give unto him that is athirst of the fountain of the water of life freely. He that overcometh shall inherit all things; and I will be his God, and he shall be my son. But the fearful, and unbelieving, and the abominable, and murderers, and whoremongers, and sorcerers, and idolaters, and all liars, shall have their part in the lake which burneth with fire and brimstone: which is the second death."

There is a place that God has "prepared for the devil and his angels." It is a place where horrors defy description and the occupants are beyond hope. Though prepared for Satan and his angels, it will be the eternal habitat of all whose names are not written in the "book of life." The name given to this place in Scripture is "Gehenna," or "hell," or "the lake of fire," but it might well be called "Eternity's Insane Asylum," for it is the everlasting abode of the spiritually insane.

Jesus told the story of a rich man who stored up his grain and goods. He enlarged his barns and engaged in hopes of sumptuous living for a great while to come. But because he made great plans for the enjoyment of this world and made no preparation for ETERNITY, Jesus called him a fool, leaving no doubt that He considered all who live and neglect preparations for a home in Heaven as SPIRITUALLY INSANE!

Sadly, there are many such in the world, and perhaps, some in this very congregation today, so my subject this morning is, "Eternity's Insane Asylum"- "The Place," "The People," and "The Program."

The Place

Re 20:15 "And whosoever was not found written in the book of life was cast into the lake of fire."

What is it like in Hell- Eternity's Insane Asylum?

A Place of Separation:

From God, His glory, and His goodness:

2Th 1:8-9 "In flaming fire taking vengeance on them that know not God, and that obey not the gospel of our Lord Jesus Christ: Who shall be punished with everlasting destruction from the presence of the Lord, and from the glory of his power;"

From Heaven:

Re 22:14-15 "Blessed *are* they that do his commandments, that they may have right to the tree of life, and may enter in through the gates into the city. For without *are* dogs, and sorcerers, and whoremongers, and murderers, and idolaters, and whosoever loveth and maketh a lie."

From the saved

From comfort:

There is no rest, no relief, no peace, no water- no good things of life in Hell.

From sinful pleasure:

There is no booze, drugs, sex, or partying in Hell.

No friendship

Many people make the foolish statement, "I want to go to Hell, since all my friends will be there." There will be no friends in Hell.

A Place of Confinement:

Eternity's insane asylum is a place of permanent confinement. There are no exits. There is no hope, or relief, or release. There are no visitation rights or privileges in Hell.

A Place of Suffering:

Physical suffering:

There are literal flames in Hell where the unsaved will burn for all eternity. There is continual weeping and wailing in Hell. There is torment of every sort in that horrible place:

Re 14:10-11 "The same shall drink of the wine of the wrath of God, which is poured out without mixture into the cup of his indignation; and he shall be tormented with fire and brimstone in the presence of the holy angels, and in the presence of the Lamb: And the smoke of their torment ascendeth up for ever and ever: and they have no rest day nor night...”

Mental Suffering:

There will be terrible mental suffering in Hell. It is a place of eternal shame, guilt, and tormenting memories. The rich man described in Luke 16 went to Hell, and in addition to the physical torment and unquenchable thirst he suffered, he remembered that he had five brethren who were on their way to that same place of torment:

Lu 16:27-28 “Then he said, I pray thee therefore, father, that thou wouldest send him to my father's house: For I have five brethren; that he may testify unto them, lest they also come into this place of torment.”

Hell is a place of physical and mental torment.

<u>The People</u>

Who will go to Hell- Eternity’s Insane Asylum?

Those Who Love Sin and Refuse to Repent:

Those mentioned in Revelation 21:8:

Re 21:8 “But the fearful, and unbelieving, and the abominable, and murderers, and whoremongers, and sorcerers, and idolaters, and all liars, shall have their part in the lake which burneth with fire and brimstone: which is the second death.”

Those mentioned by the Apostle Paul in 1 Corinthians 6:

1Co 6:9-10 “Know ye not that the unrighteous shall not inherit the kingdom of God? Be not deceived: neither fornicators, nor idolaters, nor adulterers, nor effeminate, nor abusers of themselves with mankind, Nor thieves, nor covetous, nor drunkards, nor revilers, nor extortioners, shall inherit the kingdom of God.”

Multitudes Show their Insanity Today by their Love of Sin:

I was preaching a revival in Lexie Crossroads, Tennessee. There was a young girl there who attended the service. After the service, I spoke to this young lady and asked her, "Are you a Christian?" "No," she answered. I asked her, "Would you like to be a Christian?" "No," she said. "I'm enjoying the world too much to become a Christian." This young woman was honest, but she was spiritually insane.

The Word of God tells us that the pleasure of sin is only for a season; but the payday for sin is eternal and sure. Unless you repent, and turn to Jesus Christ, your everlasting abode will be Eternity's Insane Asylum. I urge you to turn from the love of sin to the love and forgiveness of God.

Those Who Prepare for the Present, But not for Eternity:

The following article appeared in the January 18, 1960 issue of *Life* Magazine about a man named Malete G. Hanzkos, or Mike Hanzas, a man who began making arrangements for his own death:

> "Mike bought a grave plot and then inspected his property once a week. Mike meticulously trimmed the grass, and, on Memorial Day, placed a small, potted geranium on the grave. He stated, 'I want to see flowers there now. I won't be able to after I'm gone.'

> Mike next purchased a casket and a vault. 'I want to buy my new home,' he explained. When he passed the funeral home, he would stop in and see his casket: 'That's where I'm going to live someday,' he declared cheerfully. Next, he ordered a headstone, as well as his choice of flowers for the funeral.

> Then, he called his nephew, Nick Kallos and family of Dearborn, Michigan, asking them to visit him because, 'I have something to show you.' After dinner, Mike portioned

> out his personal effects, finally handing Nick his will. He took one more step, collapsed, and dropped dead of heart failure." (*Life Magazine*, January 18, 1960, pp. 31-33)
>
> A reviewer of the article wisely observed, "Mike Hanzas had apparently made every arrangement but one...He acknowledged that "it is appointed unto men once to die." Yet, he seemed oblivious of the other half of the truth, 'but after this the judgment' (Heb. 9:27)."

Some time ago, I visited a man to talk with him about his salvation. The young man was in his thirties. As I urged upon him his need to be saved, he made many excuses. He said, "I don't have time to be saved now. I'm just too busy. I have too many other responsibilities to think about that right now." Four months later, this young man found time to die. The person who puts off salvation- who prepares for the present, but not for eternity -is spiritually insane:

Jas 4:13-14 "Go to now, ye that say, To day or to morrow we will go into such a city, and continue there a year, and buy and sell, and get gain: Whereas ye know not what *shall be* on the morrow. For what *is* your life? It is even a vapour, that appeareth for a little time, and then vanisheth away."

The Person Who Deliberately Rejects Christ is Spiritually Insane:

A man once came to one of our services where I was pastor. During the service, it was clear that this man was under deep conviction, yet, he refused to repent and come to Christ. He left the service and told the lady who had invited him, "I will never be back. I won't come and have someone try and convince me to do what I don't want to do."

I tried to visit the man, but was never able to see him. He was a truck driver and was constantly away on the road. Sadly, a few weeks later, the man was killed in a traffic accident. This man refused his last opportunity to be saved. He was spiritually insane.

The Person Who Rejects God's Simple Plan of Salvation is Spiritually Insane:

God has given us the simple plan of salvation. Jesus paid the full price for all of us. Salvation is a free gift of God. To reject it is spiritual insanity.

Many depend on other ways to get to Heaven- church membership, religion, morality, baptism:

Jesus left Heaven's glory and went to the cross to suffer and pay for our sins. If we could do it ourselves, Christ did not need to come and die. But we are wretched sinners with no strength to save ourselves:

Ro 3:23 "For all have sinned, and come short of the glory of God;"

Ro 6:23 "For the wages of sin _is_ death; but the gift of God _is_ eternal life through Jesus Christ our Lord."

Christ alone is able to save us. He is the only Savior:

Joh 14:6 "Jesus saith unto him, I am the way, the truth, and the life: no man cometh unto the Father, but by me."

Ac 4:12 "Neither is there salvation in any other: for there is none other name under heaven given among men, whereby we must be saved."

Some refuse the simplicity of God's plan of salvation:

Ro 5:8 "But God commendeth his love toward us, in that, while we were yet sinners, Christ died for us."

Ro 10:9-10 "That if thou shalt confess with thy mouth the Lord Jesus, and shalt believe in thine heart that God hath raised him from the dead, thou shalt be saved. For with the heart man believeth unto righteousness; and with the mouth confession is made unto salvation."

To Live is Christ

Some wait for a certain "time" to be saved:

2Co 6:2 "(...behold, now _is_ the accepted time; behold, now _is_ the day of salvation.)"

Some seek a certain emotional feeling before trusting Christ as Savior.

God solemnly warns us not to neglect His salvation:

Heb 2:3 "How shall we escape, if we neglect so great salvation; which at the first began to be spoken by the Lord, and was confirmed unto us by them that heard _him;_"

The Program:

Who wants you to go to Eternity's Insane Asylum?

God did not Prepare Hell for Mankind:

Jesus Himself said that everlasting fire was "prepared for the devil and his angels" (Mt. 25:41). It is not God's will that any should perish, but that all should come to repentance:

2Pe 3:9 "The Lord is not slack concerning his promise, as some men count slackness; but is longsuffering to us-ward, not willing that any should perish, but that all should come to repentance."

God does not want you to go there. He wants all men to be saved:

1Ti 2:3-4 "For this _is_ good and acceptable in the sight of God our Saviour; Who will have all men to be saved, and to come unto the knowledge of the truth."

God through His Son, Jesus Christ, has made it possible for all to be saved. Jesus Christ paid the full redemption price for sinners. He does not want you to go to Hell:

Joh 3:16 "For God so loved the world, that he gave his only begotten Son, that whosoever believeth in him should not perish, but have everlasting life."

God's people in the church do not want you to go to Hell. The Holy Spirit of God does not want you to go there. He calls to you to come. He is drawing you to come to Jesus Christ:

Re 22:17 "And the Spirit and the bride say, Come. And let him that heareth say, Come. And let him that is athirst come. And whosoever will, let him take the water of life freely."

If you go to Hell, you'll have to go over God's love, around the cross, resisting the Holy Spirit, and in spite of the concerned prayers of Christians in the church. You do not want to spend eternity in such a place!

It is Satan and his angels who want you in this eternal asylum of the damned!

But you must decide. The choice is yours. Will you continue in your spiritual insanity until it is too late?

"Oh, Why Not Tonight"

Oh, do not let the Word depart,

And close thine eyes against the light;

Poor sinner, harden not your heart,

Be saved, oh, tonight.

Refrain:

Oh, why not tonight?

Oh, why not tonight?

Wilt thou be saved?

Then why not tonight?

Tomorrow's sun may never rise

To bless thy long-deluded sight;

This is the time, oh, then be wise,

Be saved, oh, tonight.

Oh, why not tonight?

Oh, why not tonight?

Wilt thou be saved?

Then why not tonight?

Our Lord in pity lingers still,

And wilt thou thus His love requite?

Renounce at once thy stubborn will,

Be saved, oh, tonight.

Oh, why not tonight?

Oh, why not tonight?

Wilt thou be saved?

Then why not tonight?

Our blessed Lord refuses none

Who would to Him their souls unite;

Believe on Him, the work is done,

Be saved, oh, tonight.

Oh, why not tonight?

Oh, why not tonight?

Wilt thou be saved?

Then why not tonight?

-Elizabeth H. Reed, 1842

Chapter 11

"Heaven- Where it is, What it will be Like, and Who will be There"

(Preached on May 10, 1979)

Re 21:1-5 "And I saw a new heaven and a new earth: for the first heaven and the first earth were passed away; and there was no more sea. And I John saw the holy city, new Jerusalem, coming down from God out of heaven, prepared as a bride adorned for her husband. And I heard a great voice out of heaven saying, Behold, the tabernacle of God *is* with men, and he will dwell with them, and they shall be his people, and God himself shall be with them, *and be* their God. And God shall wipe away all tears from their eyes; and there shall be no more death, neither sorrow, nor crying, neither shall there be any more pain: for the former things are passed away. And he that sat upon the throne said, Behold, I make all things new. And he said unto me, Write: for these words are true and faithful."

Re 22:1-5 "And he shewed me a pure river of water of life, clear as crystal, proceeding out of the throne of God and of the Lamb. In the midst of the street of it, and on either side of the river, *was there* the tree of life, which bare twelve *manner of* fruits, *and* yielded her fruit every month: and the leaves of the tree *were* for the healing of the nations. And there shall be no more curse: but the throne of God and of the Lamb shall be in it; and his servants shall serve him: And they shall see his face; and his name *shall be* in their foreheads. And there shall be no night there; and they need no candle, neither light of the sun; for the Lord God giveth them light: and they shall reign for ever and ever."

Heaven should be dear to the heart of every Christian. It is there that every true believer will spend the endless ages of eternity. It is in that place that all of our saved loved ones have gone to await our arrival and that glad day of their coming with Jesus Christ. In Heaven, every little baby who has ever died enjoys the brightness of eternal day. It is in Heaven that our blessed Savior sits at God's right hand awaiting the day of His glorious return.

Heaven's Location- Where is it?

Heaven is Above Us:

Jesus came down from Heaven and returned up back to Heaven:

Joh 3:12-13 "If I have told you earthly things, and ye believe not, how shall ye believe, if I tell you *of* heavenly things? And no man hath ascended up to heaven, but he that came down from heaven, *even* the Son of man which is in heaven."

Joh 6:33 "For the bread of God is he which cometh down from heaven, and giveth life unto the world."

Joh 6:38 "For I came down from heaven, not to do mine own will, but the will of him that sent me."

Lu 24:50-51 "And he led them out as far as to Bethany, and he lifted up his hands, and blessed them. And it came to pass, while he blessed them, he was parted from them, and carried up into heaven."

Jesus, at His second coming, will descend from Heaven with His saints:

Re 19:11, 14 And I saw heaven opened, and behold a white horse; and he that sat upon him *was* called Faithful and True, and in righteousness he doth judge and make war...And the armies *which were* in heaven followed him upon white horses, clothed in fine linen, white and clean."

Heaven is Where God Is:

Heaven is the dwelling place of Almighty God, the place where God reigns supreme. When Jesus spoke to His disciples of Heaven, He called it "My Father's House," a place of "many mansions" where He is preparing a place for us:

Joh 14:2-3 "In my Father's house are many mansions: if *it were* not *so*, I would have told you. I go to prepare a place for you. And if I go and prepare a place for you, I will come again, and receive you unto myself; that where I am, *there* ye may be also."

Wherever God is, it is Heaven. Heaven is a place filled with the love, holiness, and goodness of God. Jesus exemplified the goodness and love of God when He walked upon the earth:

Mt 15:30-31 "And great multitudes came unto him, having with them *those that were* lame, blind, dumb, maimed, and many others, and cast them down at Jesus' feet; and he healed them: Insomuch that the multitude wondered, when they saw the dumb to speak, the maimed to be whole, the lame to walk, and the blind to see: and they glorified the God of Israel."

Heaven is the Place of God's Throne:

Many Scriptures tell us that Heaven is the place of God's throne. It is the place where God reigns over this universe:

Ps 45:6 "Thy throne, O God, *is* for ever and ever: the sceptre of thy kingdom *is* a right sceptre."

Ps 93:1-2 "The LORD reigneth, he is clothed with majesty; the LORD is clothed with strength, *wherewith* he hath girded himself: the world also is stablished, that it cannot be moved. Thy throne *is* established of old: thou *art* from everlasting."

The prophet Isaiah described his vision of God upon His throne:

Isa 6:1-3 "In the year that king Uzziah died I saw also the Lord sitting upon a throne, high and lifted up, and his train filled the temple. Above it stood the seraphims: each one had six wings; with twain he covered his face, and with twain he covered his feet, and with twain he did fly. And one cried unto another, and said, Holy, holy, holy, *is* the LORD of hosts: the whole earth *is* full of his glory."

The Apostle John described God's throne set in Heaven:

Re 4:2-3 "And immediately I was in the spirit: and, behold, a throne was set in heaven, and *one* sat on the throne. And he that sat was to look upon like a jasper and a sardine stone: and *there was* a rainbow round about the throne, in sight like unto an emerald."

Heaven is the Place Where Christ is Seated at God's Right Hand:

Lu 22:69 "Hereafter shall the Son of man sit on the right hand of the power of God."

Mr 16:19 "So then after the Lord had spoken unto them, he was received up into heaven, and sat on the right hand of God."

Ac 2:33 "Therefore being by the right hand of God exalted, and having received of the Father the promise of the Holy Ghost, he hath shed forth this, which ye now see and hear."

Ac 5:31 "Him hath God exalted with his right hand *to be* a Prince and a Saviour, for to give repentance to Israel, and forgiveness of sins."

Col 3:1 "If ye then be risen with Christ, seek those things which are above, where Christ sitteth on the right hand of God."

Heb 10:12 "But this man, after he had offered one sacrifice for sins for ever, sat down on the right hand of God;"

There at the right hand of God, Jesus Christ is our Great High Priest and Intercessor:

Heb 12:2 "Looking unto Jesus the author and finisher of *our* faith; who for the joy that was set before him endured the cross, despising the shame, and is set down at the right hand of the throne of God."

Ro 8:34 Who *is* he that condemneth? *It is* Christ that died, yea rather, that is risen again, who is even at the right hand of God, who also maketh intercession for us.

Heb 7:24-26 "But this *man*, because he continueth ever, hath an unchangeable priesthood. Wherefore he is able also to save them to the uttermost that come unto God by him, seeing he ever liveth to make intercession for them. For such an high priest became us, *who is* holy, harmless, undefiled, separate from sinners, and made higher than the heavens;"

There at God's right hand, Jesus Christ receives His dear ones into glory:

Ac 7:55-56, 59 "But he, being full of the Holy Ghost, looked up stedfastly into heaven, and saw the glory of God, and Jesus standing on the right hand of God, And said, Behold, I see the heavens opened, and the Son of man standing on the right hand of God...And they stoned Stephen, calling upon *God*, and saying, Lord Jesus, receive my spirit."

Jesus Christ not only sends His angels to gather His dear ones, but He stands ready to greet and receive His own. And He guarantees our entrance into Heaven by His own blood!

Heaven's Description- What is it Like?

Heaven is A Place:

Heaven is a literal location. Jesus said, "I go to prepare a **place** for you." Abraham looked for the Heavenly "city."- a literal city, built by God:

Heb 11:9-10 "By faith he sojourned in the land of promise, as *in* a strange country, dwelling in tabernacles with Isaac and Jacob, the heirs with him of the same promise: For he looked for a city which hath foundations, whose builder and maker *is* God."

That city is described in detail in Revelation 21:

Re 21:10-27 "And he carried me away in the spirit to a great and high mountain, and shewed me that great city, the holy Jerusalem, descending out of heaven from God, Having the glory of God: and her light *was* like unto a stone most precious, even like a jasper stone, clear as crystal; And had a wall great and high, *and* had twelve gates, and at the gates twelve angels, and names written thereon, which are *the names* of the twelve tribes of the children of Israel: On the east three gates; on the north three gates; on the south three gates; and on the west three gates. And the wall of the city had twelve foundations, and in them the names of the twelve apostles of the Lamb. And he that talked with me had a golden reed to measure the city, and the gates thereof, and the wall thereof. And the city lieth foursquare, and the length is as large as the breadth: and he measured the city with the reed, twelve thousand furlongs. The length and the breadth and the height of it are equal. And he measured the wall thereof, an hundred *and* forty *and* four cubits, *according to* the measure of a man, that is, of the angel. And the building of the wall of it was *of* jasper: and the city *was* pure gold, like unto clear glass. And the foundations of the wall of the city *were* garnished with all manner of precious stones. The first foundation *was* jasper; the second, sapphire; the third, a chalcedony; the fourth, an emerald; The fifth, sardonyx; the sixth, sardius; the seventh, chrysolite; the eighth, beryl; the ninth, a topaz; the tenth, a chrysoprasus; the eleventh, a jacinth; the twelfth, an amethyst. And the twelve gates *were* twelve pearls; every several gate was of one pearl: and the street of the city *was* pure gold, as it were transparent glass. And I saw no temple therein: for the Lord God Almighty and the Lamb are the temple of it. And the city had no need of the sun, neither of the moon, to shine in it: for the glory of God did lighten it, and the Lamb *is* the light thereof. And the nations of them which are saved shall walk in the light of it: and the kings of the earth do bring their glory and honour into it. And the gates of it shall not be shut at all by day: for there shall be no night there. And they shall bring the glory and honour of the nations into it. And there shall in no wise enter into it any thing that defileth, neither *whatsoever* worketh abomination, or *maketh* a lie: but they which are written in the Lamb's book of life."

Heaven is a Place of Beauty and Splendor:

Form this description in Revelation 21, we read of the beauty and splendor of the Heavenly city that Christ is preparing for the redeemed. The measurements given teach us that the city is a square that is fifteen hundred miles wide and high. It has twelve gates, each made of a single pearl. It has twelve foundations made of precious stones. It has walls made of jasper and streets made of pure, translucent gold. Heaven is the most beautiful city ever imagined. It is glorious!

Heaven is a Place of Complete Victory and Glorious Triumph:

In this life, we have trouble, just as Jesus said we would:

Joh 16:33 "These things I have spoken unto you, that in me ye might have peace. In the world ye shall have tribulation: but be of good cheer; I have overcome the world."

We have spiritual warfare and struggles in this world:

2Co 7:1 "Having therefore these promises, dearly beloved, let us cleanse ourselves from all filthiness of the flesh and spirit, perfecting holiness in the fear of God."

Eph 6:12 "For we wrestle not against flesh and blood, but against principalities, against powers, against the rulers of the darkness of this world, against spiritual wickedness in high *places.*"

In this life, we can expect suffering, trouble, burdens, tears, and even failure. But in Heaven, all will be victory and blessing.

Heaven is a Place of Rest from Labor:

In Heaven, there will be no more weakness, no more burdens, no more weariness, and no more sleepless nights- only eternal rest and peace.

Heaven is a Place of Unspeakable Joy:

We have a foretaste of that joy in this life as we walk with Christ. We glory in His presence here with joy unspeakable as we get a glimpse of His wonder and love. We have fellowship with God's people here and receive a taste of Heaven in that. But oh, the joy we shall have when we are all united in His presence in glory! Peter wrote of the sweet joy we who love Christ have in this life; but what joy we will have when we receive "the end of our faith," and see our Savior face to face in glory:

1Pe 1:6-9 "Wherein ye greatly rejoice, though now for a season, if need be, ye are in heaviness through manifold temptations: That the trial of your faith, being much more precious than of gold that perisheth, though it be tried with fire, might be found unto praise and honour and glory at the appearing of Jesus Christ: Whom having not seen, ye love; in whom, though now ye see *him* not, yet believing, ye rejoice with joy unspeakable and full of glory: Receiving the end of your faith, *even* the salvation of *your* souls."

"Oh, That Will Be Glory"

When all my labors and trials are o'er,

And I am safe on that beautiful shore,

Just to be near the dear Lord I adore,

Will through the ages be glory for me.

Refrain:

Oh, that will be glory for me,

Glory for me, glory for me,

When by His grace I shall look on His face,

That will be glory, be glory for me.

When, by the gift of His infinite grace,

I am accorded in heaven a place,

Just to be there and to look on His face,

Will through the ages be glory for me.

Friends will be there I have loved long ago;

Joy like a river around me will flow;

Yet just a smile from my Savior, I know,

Will through the ages be glory for me.

Refrain:

Oh, that will be glory for me,

Glory for me, glory for me,

When by His grace I shall look on His face,

That will be glory, be glory for me.

-Charles H. Gabriel, pub.1900

Heaven is a Place of Peace:

What will it be like to be in a place where there is complete peace- free from worry, care, fear, and conflict? That will truly be Heaven.

Heaven is a Place of Complete, Unmarred Fellowship:

Fellowship with God:

Oh, the joy of unbroken, unhindered fellowship with God! The psalmist David described such joy in Psalm 119:

Ps 119:1-2 "Blessed *are* the undefiled in the way, who walk in the law of the LORD. Blessed *are* they that keep his testimonies, *and that* seek him with the whole heart."

But so often our fellowship with God is broken here by our own unfaithfulness. David too lamented that fact:

Ps 119:5-6 "O that my ways were directed to keep thy statutes! Then shall I not be ashamed, when I have respect unto all thy commandments."

Our greatest joy here comes as we follow our Savior in obedience through the power of the Holy Spirit. But in Heaven, we will know the sweetness of unhindered and unbroken fellowship with God.

Fellowship with others:

In Heaven, there will be no broken relationships, no hurt feelings, no envy, or pride. We will enjoy sweet communion with one another in the presence of our Savior who loved and forgave us through His shed blood.

A place of sweet reunion:

Oh, what a joyous reunion we will have in Heaven with our loved ones and friends who have gone on before us. Old acquaintances will be renewed. Sweet relations will be restored. We will enjoy a joyous fellowship with all the believers who have gone on before us.

A place of recognition:

The question is often asked, "Will I know my loved ones in Heaven?" The answer is decidedly, "Yes!" The disciples knew Jesus after He was raised from the dead. They also recognized Moses and Elijah on the mount of Transfiguration even though they had never seen them before. Even in hell there is recognition. The rich man of Luke 16 knew Lazarus when he saw him in Abraham's bosom. David looked forward to seeing his little son who had died (2 Sa. 12:23). Stephen, as he was dying, recognized Jesus standing in Heaven. Many a dying saint has seen and recognized the Lord Jesus and other loved ones in their departing hour. Paul spoke of the knowledge we will have when we see the light of eternal day in Heaven:

1Co 13:12 "For now we see through a glass, darkly; but then face to face: now I know in part; but then shall I know even as also I am known."

Heaven Is a Place of Uninterrupted Service:

In this life, our service for God is often hindered by our own weakness, by circumstances, or by spiritual warfare. But in Heaven, we, like the redeemed saints of the coming Tribulation period described in Revelation 7, will serve God day and night in all the fullness of His strength:

Re 7:14-15 "And I said unto him, Sir, thou knowest. And he said to me, These are they which came out of great tribulation, and have washed their robes, and made them white in the blood of the Lamb. Therefore are they before the throne of God, and serve him day and night in his temple: and he that sitteth on the throne shall dwell among them."

Heaven Is a Place of Holiness:

Heaven is a place of holiness. There will be no sin there. There, as described in Isaiah's vision, the seraphim cry, "Holy, holy, holy." Nothing which defiles will ever enter that Heavenly city prepared of God for His own:

Re 21:27 "And there shall in no wise enter into it any thing that defileth, neither *whatsoever* worketh abomination, or *maketh* a lie..."

Nothing filthy, suggestive, lude, vile, perverted, immodest, or immoral will enter there. Nothing selfish, vain, proud, or dishonest- nothing of the sinful flesh, nothing of Satan, nothing of this fallen world -will be there.

Heaven is a Place of Glory:

It is Lightened by the Glory of God:

Re 21:23 "And the city had no need of the sun, neither of the moon, to shine in it: for the glory of God did lighten it, and the Lamb *is* the light thereof."

The Saints will Share that Glory:

Ro 8:17-18 "And if children, then heirs; heirs of God, and joint-heirs with Christ; if so be that we suffer with *him*, that we may be also glorified together. For I reckon that the sufferings of this present time *are* not worthy *to be compared* with the glory which shall be revealed in us."

2Ti 2:12 "If we suffer, we shall also reign with *him*..."

The Saints will Reflect that Glory:

Da 12:3 "And they that be wise shall shine as the brightness of the firmament; and they that turn many to righteousness as the stars for ever and ever."

Eph 3:21 "Unto him *be* glory in the church by Christ Jesus throughout all ages, world without end. Amen."

Re 21:2 "And I John saw the holy city, new Jerusalem, coming down from God out of heaven, prepared as a bride adorned for her husband."

Heaven- Who Will Be There?

Those Who Are Born Again Will Be There:

Joh 3:3-5 "Jesus answered and said unto him, Verily, verily, I say unto thee, Except a man be born again, he cannot see the kingdom of God. Nicodemus saith unto him, How can a man be born when he is old? can he enter the second time into his mother's womb, and be born? Jesus answered, Verily, verily, I say unto thee, Except a man be born of water and *of* the Spirit, he cannot enter into the kingdom of God."

Only those who are born again through the Holy Spirit of God by faith in the Son of God will enter into Heaven.

Those Who Are Washed in the Blood of the Lamb:

These too are the same born again believers. They are born again through faith in the work of Jesus Christ upon the cross of Calvary for salvation and are washed in the blood of the Lamb:

Re 7:14 "...And he said to me, These are they which came out of great tribulation, and have washed their robes, and made them white in the blood of the Lamb."

1Pe 1:18-19 "Forasmuch as ye know that ye were not redeemed with corruptible things, *as* silver and gold, from your vain conversation *received* by tradition from your fathers; But with the precious blood of Christ, as of a lamb without blemish and without spot:"

Those Whose Names are Written in the Lamb's Book of Life:

Jesus told His disciples:

Lu 10:20 "Notwithstanding in this rejoice not, that the spirits are subject unto you; but rather rejoice, because your names are written in heaven."

Their names were written in Heaven because they, with the exception of Judas Iscariot, had believed on the Christ whom the Father had sent:

Joh 6:68-69 "Then Simon Peter answered him, Lord, to whom shall we go? thou hast the words of eternal life. And we believe and are sure that thou art that Christ, the Son of the living God."

The names of unbelievers are not found in the book of life. Only those whose names are written there will enter Heaven:

Re 13:8 "And all that dwell upon the earth shall worship him, whose names are not written in the book of life of the Lamb slain from the foundation of the world."

Re 20:15 "And whosoever was not found written in the book of life was cast into the lake of fire."

Only Those Who Have Received Christ By Faith Will Enter Heaven:

Joh 1:12 "But as many as received him, to them gave he power to become the sons of God, *even* to them that believe on his name:"

Joh 5:24 "Verily, verily, I say unto you, He that heareth my word, and believeth on him that sent me, hath everlasting life, and shall not come into condemnation; but is passed from death unto life."

In conclusion, Jesus is preparing a place for all those who trust Him by faith for salvation. He is coming again to receive those dear ones unto Himself, that where He is, there we may be also. Have you made your reservation for Heaven?

"Only Trust Him"

Come, every soul by sin oppressed,

There's mercy with the Lord,

And He will surely give you rest

By trusting in His Word.

Refrain:

Only trust Him, only trust Him,

Only trust Him now;

He will save you, He will save you,

He will save you now.

For Jesus shed His precious blood

Rich blessings to bestow;

Plunge now into the crimson flood

That washes white as snow.

Yes, Jesus is the truth, the way,

That leads you into rest;

Believe in Him without delay

And you are fully blest.

Come, then, and join this holy band,

And on to glory go,

To dwell in that celestial land

Where joys immortal flow.

Refrain:

Only trust Him, only trust Him,

Only trust Him now;

He will save you, He will save you,

He will save you now.

-John H. Stockton, bef.1873

Chapter 12

"Are You Ready For Jesus To Come?"
(Preached December 27, 1992)

Ac 1:1, 4-11 "The former treatise have I made, O Theophilus, of all that Jesus began both to do and teach...And, being assembled together with *them*, commanded them that they should not depart from Jerusalem, but wait for the promise of the Father, which, *saith he*, ye have heard of me. For John truly baptized with water; but ye shall be baptized with the Holy Ghost not many days hence. When they therefore were come together, they asked of him, saying, Lord, wilt thou at this time restore again the kingdom to Israel? And he said unto them, It is not for you to know the times or the seasons, which the Father hath put in his own power. But ye shall receive power, after that the Holy Ghost is come upon you: and ye shall be witnesses unto me both in Jerusalem, and in all Judaea, and in Samaria, and unto the uttermost part of the earth. And when he had spoken these things, while they beheld, he was taken up; and a cloud received him out of their sight. And while they looked stedfastly toward heaven as he went up, behold, two men stood by them in white apparel; Which also said, Ye men of Galilee, why stand ye gazing up into heaven? this same Jesus, which is taken up from you into heaven, shall so come in like manner as ye have seen him go into heaven."

I want to ask you a serious question today- Are you ready for Jesus to come again? Some years ago, in 1988, someone put out a book citing eighty-eight reasons why Jesus would come again in 1988. This man set a particular date and said that Jesus would come on that day in 1988. Lots of folks got excited, and not a few even made professions of getting saved. Hopefully, some of those really were saved. But the truth is, nobody knows when Jesus Christ is coming again. Concerning the time of His coming, Jesus said:

Mt 24:35-37 "Heaven and earth shall pass away, but my words shall not pass away. But of that day and hour knoweth no *man*, no, not the angels of heaven, but my

Father only. But as the days of Noe *were*, so shall also the coming of the Son of man be."

We can be absolutely sure of the fact that Jesus will come again. He will come as His Word promises:

1Th 4:16 "For the Lord himself shall descend from heaven with a shout, with the voice of the archangel, and with the trump of God..."

We all need to be ready for that glorious event! Are you ready for Jesus to come? I want us to consider it under four points: The Promise of His Coming, The Person of His Coming, The Plan for His Coming, and The Preparation for His Coming:

The Promise of His Coming:

Ac 1:10-11 "And while they looked stedfastly toward heaven as he went up, behold, two men stood by them in white apparel; Which also said, Ye men of Galilee, why stand ye gazing up into heaven? **this same Jesus, which is taken up from you into heaven, shall so come in like manner as ye have seen him go into heaven.**"

The Second Coming of Jesus Christ is Sure:

The disciples were watching Jesus as He ascended up to Heaven in His glorified body. I don't know what they were thinking, but I am sure they were filled with wonder and awe. They had walked with Jesus for three years. They had seen Him perform wondrous miracles. Some had watched Christ die upon the cross. They had watched as He hung there in agony and shame. Some had participated in His burial. And all had witnessed His miraculous resurrection from the dead as He appeared to them at various times and places over a period of forty days. Now, they watched with wonder and amazement as He ascended into the heavens in a cloud of glory.

As they watched and wondered, they were suddenly challenged by the appearance of two men in white apparel speaking to them and reminding them of a promise and a purpose. The promise was the sure return of Jesus Christ in glory, and the purpose was to occupy until He comes again- to busy themselves with the work He commissioned them to do (Mt. 28:19-20).

The Scriptures Clearly Promise the Glorious Return of Christ:

David predicted it in Psalm 102:

Ps 102:15-16 "So the heathen shall fear the name of the LORD, and all the kings of the earth thy glory. When the LORD shall build up Zion, he shall appear in his glory."

Enoch predicted it:

Jude 1:14-15 "And Enoch also, the seventh from Adam, prophesied of these, saying, Behold, the Lord cometh with ten thousands of his saints, To execute judgment upon all, and to convince all that are ungodly among them of all their ungodly deeds which they have ungodly committed, and of all their hard *speeches* which ungodly sinners have spoken against him."

Daniel prophesied of Christ's return:

Da 7:13 "I saw in the night visions, and, behold, *one* like the Son of man came with the clouds of heaven, and came to the Ancient of days, and they brought him near before him."

Zechariah declared the certain return of Jesus Christ to the Mount of Olives as King:

Zec 14:4 "And his feet shall stand in that day upon the mount of Olives, which *is* before Jerusalem on the east, and the mount of Olives shall cleave in the midst thereof toward the east and toward the west, *and there shall be* a very great valley; and half of the mountain shall remove toward the north, and half of it toward the south."

Zec 14:9 "And the LORD shall be king over all the earth: in that day shall there be one LORD, and his name one."

Jesus, Himself, promised that He would return:

Joh 14:2-4 "In my Father's house are many mansions: if *it were* not *so*, I would have told you. I go to prepare a place for you. And if I go and prepare a place for you, I will come again, and receive you unto myself; that where I am, *there* ye may be also."

Mt 24:44 "Therefore be ye also ready: for in such an hour as ye think not the Son of man cometh."

Throughout the New Testament, the promise is continued with one verse in every twenty-five speaking in some way concerning the coming of our living Lord, Jesus Christ:

Tit 2:13 "Looking for that blessed hope, and the glorious appearing of the great God and our Saviour Jesus Christ;"

1Th 4:16-17 "For the Lord himself shall descend from heaven with a shout, with the voice of the archangel, and with the trump of God: and the dead in Christ shall rise first: Then we which are alive *and* remain shall be caught up together with them in the clouds, to meet the Lord in the air: and so shall we ever be with the Lord."

The Second Coming of Jesus Christ is Imminent:

As we read in Matthew 24:44, we are to look for Christ's coming. We are to be ready for it, because it could happen any day, and at any moment.

We are to love His appearing:

2Ti 4:8 "Henceforth there is laid up for me a crown of righteousness, which the Lord, the righteous judge, shall give me at that day: and not to me only, but unto all them also that love his appearing."

We are to purify ourselves as He is pure as we wait for His coming:

1Jo 3:2-3 "Beloved, now are we the sons of God, and it doth not yet appear what we shall be: but we know that, when he shall appear, we shall be like him; for we shall see him as he is. And every man that hath this hope in him purifieth himself, even as he is pure."

Christ's return is the Christian's "blessed hope":

Tit 2:13 "Looking for that blessed hope, and the glorious appearing of the great God and our Saviour Jesus Christ;"

We are to watch for Christ's return with a serious mind:

1Th 5:6 "Therefore let us not sleep, as *do* others; but let us watch and be sober."

We are to pray for Christ's return:

Lu 11:2 "And he said unto them, When ye pray, say, Our Father which art in heaven, Hallowed be thy name. **Thy kingdom come**. Thy will be done, as in heaven, so in earth."

We ought to hasten His coming through prayer and our witness for Jesus Christ:

2Pe 3:11-12 "*Seeing* then *that* all these things shall be dissolved, what manner *of persons* ought ye to be in *all* holy conversation and godliness, Looking for and hasting unto the coming of the day of God, wherein the heavens being on fire shall be dissolved, and the elements shall melt with fervent heat?"

The Time of Christ's Coming is Unknown, But Apparently Near:

There are no signs preceding the Rapture of the Church- the first phase of Christ's coming. Christ's coming in the air for His own is imminent and could happen at any moment. But there are many signs that will be fulfilled during the Tribulation period- the seven year period of God's judgment prior to Christ's return to the earth.

During the Tribulation, there will be famines, earthquakes, and pestilence that will increase in number and intensity. There will be the rise of the global government that will be a revived form of the Roman Empire. The rise of a United Europe, along with events in Russia and Israel, may well be the beginning stages of this global government under the rule of the Antichrist.

But, as Christians, we do not need to be so much concerned about signs, but rather, we should be focused upon the Person who is coming- Jesus Christ.

The Person of His Coming:

Acts 1:11 tells us, that "this same Jesus…shall so come in like manner as ye have seen Him go into Heaven."

What We Are Looking for is the Coming of a Person:

It is the Person who was born in Bethlehem and laid in a manger.

It is the Person who walked through the streets of Jerusalem and the cities of Galilee performing mighty miracles and proclaiming God's Word.

It is the Person, who died for our sins and arose from the grave.

It is the Person who appeared in His glorified body to His "little flock" (Lu. 12:32) of followers, and then ascended into glory to sit at the Father's right hand.

It is the Person who lives in the body of every born again, blood-washed believer to empower them for service and transform them into His likeness.

It is this Same Person Who is Coming Again:

It is that One who is our life:

Col 3:1-4 "If ye then be risen with Christ, seek those things which are above, where Christ sitteth on the right hand of God. Set your affection on things above, not on things on the earth. For ye are dead, and your life is hid with Christ in God. When Christ, *who is* our life, shall appear, then shall ye also appear with him in glory."

Hebrews 13:8 says, "Jesus Christ the same yesterday, and to day, and for ever."

This same Jesus is coming again!

The Jesus who is coming again is the one who went away.

He is the One who sent His Spirit into our hearts to cry, "Abba, Father" (Ro. 8:15).

He is the One who intercedes at God's right hand as we pray.

He is the One who is our Divine Advocate- ever pleading our case before the Father.

He is the One who makes us acceptable to the Father.

This same Jesus will come in power and great glory to rule the earth with a "rod of iron" and smite His enemies with the sword of His mouth. Listen, people, we are not so much looking for signs. We are looking for the Son!

Perhaps some of you remember some years ago when Alabama senator, Jeremiah Denton, returned to the United States after being a prisoner of war in Vietnam. Finally free, he arrived home to his native soil. When he stepped off the plane, it was a moving event as he was greeted by his little girl who leaped to hug him around his neck, and his wife fell into the arms of her husband who had finally returned, alive and safe. What joy! They had a most precious person back with them again. They were not looking for a media event. They were looking for and joyfully anticipating the reunion with a person very dear to them.

So it must be with us if we are to be prepared for the coming of Jesus our blessed Redeemer. We must focus on the Person who is coming!

The Plan for His Coming:

Ac 1:11 "...this same Jesus, which is taken up from you into heaven, shall so come in like manner as ye have seen him go into heaven."

He is Coming for the Same People:

The Rapture of the Church is the next event on God's prophetic program. No unbelievers were gathered there to see Jesus ascend into Heaven. Only believers were witnesses of Christ's resurrection and ascension into glory. Only saved people whose sins were under Jesus' blood and who hearts were transformed by His power were gathered to watch Him go into Heaven. And it will be believers who Jesus will come for when He returns.

If you are saved, you have one of two possible experiences awaiting you when Jesus comes again:

Resurrection: The Dead in Christ

-Or-

Transformation: Those Still Living When He Returns

1Th 4:14-17 "For if we believe that Jesus died and rose again, even so them also which sleep in Jesus will God bring with him. For this we say unto you by the word of the Lord, that we which are alive *and* remain unto the coming of the Lord shall not prevent them which are asleep. For the Lord himself shall descend from heaven with a shout, with the voice of the archangel, and with the trump of God: and the dead in Christ shall rise first: Then we which are alive *and* remain shall be caught up together with them in the clouds, to meet the Lord in the air: and so shall we ever be with the Lord."

1Co 15:52 "In a moment, in the twinkling of an eye, at the last trump: for the trumpet shall sound, and the dead shall be raised incorruptible, and we shall be changed."

What a glory day that will be when Jesus comes for His bride. He will come with a shout, and the dead will be raised with incorruptible bodies. Imagine the scene all over the world- from cemeteries and sepulchers, from ocean floors and desert sands, as sleeping saints will rise in resurrection glory! Then those who are alive and saved by God's grace will be transformed and translated to the skies to meet

Him and all the saints of all the ages in the air- in glory! The saved will be translated from their homes, from automobiles, from factories and places of business, from airplanes, etc. As a result, there will be great confusion and consternation upon the earth.

He is Coming to the Same Place:

When Jesus Christ returns to earth after the seven year Tribulation period, He will return with His own to the same place He left them the first time. He is coming back to Jerusalem, back to the Mount of Olives, just as Zechariah prophesied. He is coming to reign upon the throne of David- to rule and to reign upon the earth, and to destroy every enemy:

Re 19:11, 14-16 "And I saw heaven opened, and behold a white horse; and he that sat upon him *was* called Faithful and True, and in righteousness he doth judge and make war...And the armies *which were* in heaven followed him upon white horses, clothed in fine linen, white and clean. And out of his mouth goeth a sharp sword, that with it he should smite the nations: and he shall rule them with a rod of iron: and he treadeth the winepress of the fierceness and wrath of Almighty God. And he hath on *his* vesture and on his thigh a name written, KING OF KINGS, AND LORD OF LORDS."

Isa 9:6-7 "For unto us a child is born, unto us a son is given: and the government shall be upon his shoulder: and his name shall be called Wonderful, Counseller, The mighty God, The everlasting Father, The Prince of Peace. Of the increase of *his* government and peace *there shall be* no end, upon the throne of David, and upon his kingdom, to order it, and to establish it with judgment and with justice from henceforth even for ever. The zeal of the LORD of hosts will perform this."

Isa 2:4 "And he shall judge among the nations, and shall rebuke many people: and they shall beat their swords into plowshares, and their spears into pruninghooks: nation shall not lift up sword against nation, neither shall they learn war any more."

1Co 15:24-25 "Then *cometh* the end, when he shall have delivered up the kingdom to God, even the Father; when he shall have put down all rule and all authority and power. For he must reign, till he hath put all enemies under his feet."

And sorrow and sighing shall flee away:

Isa 35:10 "And the ransomed of the LORD shall return, and come to Zion with songs and everlasting joy upon their heads: they shall obtain joy and gladness, and sorrow and sighing shall flee away."

Someday, the Lion of the Tribe of Judah is going to return to Jerusalem. What a glory day it will be when Jesus comes to reign as King of kings and Lord of lords!

The Preparation for His Coming:

As Jesus ascended into Heaven, the disciples were asked, "Why stand ye gazing up into heaven?" Jesus had told them:

Ac 1:7-8 "...It is not for you to know the times or the seasons, which the Father hath put in his own power. But ye shall receive power, after that the Holy Ghost is come upon you: and ye shall be witnesses unto me both in Jerusalem, and in all Judaea, and in Samaria, and unto the uttermost part of the earth."

Jesus had left His disciples in the world for a purpose. If we are going to be ready for Christ to come, we must:

-Be His Witnesses

-Help Prepare Other Believers for His Coming

-Live Lives that Testify to His Power and Grace as Acts 1:8 Commands Us

-Not Forsake the Assembling of Ourselves Together in the Churches:

Heb 10:25 "Not forsaking the assembling of ourselves together, as the manner of some *is*; but exhorting *one another*: and so much the more, as ye see **the day** approaching."

-Live in Purity

-Live in Watchfulness and Prayer:

Lu 21:36 "Watch ye therefore, and pray always, that ye may be accounted worthy to escape all these things that shall come to pass, and to stand before the Son of man."

-Patiently Endure Trials

And finally, we also give an earnest warning to the unsaved. Turn to Christ and be saved before it is too late. Remember the words of Jesus:

Mt 24:44 "Therefore be ye also ready: for in such an hour as ye think not the Son of man cometh."

"Christ Returneth"

It may be at morn, when the day is awaking,

When sunlight through darkness and shadow is breaking,

That Jesus will come in the fullness of glory

To receive from the world "His own."

Refrain:

O Lord Jesus, how long, how long

Ere we shout the glad song—

Christ returneth! Hallelujah!

Hallelujah! Amen.

Hallelujah! Amen.

It may be at midday, it may be at twilight,

It may be, perchance, that the blackness of midnight

Will burst into light in the blaze of His glory,

When Jesus receives "His own."

Refrain:

O Lord Jesus, how long, how long

Ere we shout the glad song—

Christ returneth! Hallelujah!

Hallelujah! Amen.

Hallelujah! Amen.

While hosts cry Hosanna, from heaven descending,

With glorified saints and the angels attending,

With grace on His brow, like a halo of glory,

Will Jesus receive "His own."

Refrain:

O Lord Jesus, how long, how long

Ere we shout the glad song—

Christ returneth! Hallelujah!

Hallelujah! Amen.

Hallelujah! Amen.

Oh, joy! oh, delight! should we go without dying,

No sickness, no sadness, no dread and no crying;

Caught up through the clouds with our Lord into glory,

When Jesus receives "His own."

Refrain:

O Lord Jesus, how long, how long

Ere we shout the glad song—

Christ returneth! Hallelujah!

Hallelujah! Amen.

Hallelujah! Amen.

-H. L. Turner, pub.1878

Chapter 13

"Strangers and Gray Hairs"
(Preached April 14, 1997)

Ho 7:1-16 "When I would have healed Israel, then the iniquity of Ephraim was discovered, and the wickedness of Samaria: for they commit falsehood; and the thief cometh in, *and* the troop of robbers spoileth without. And they consider not in their hearts *that* I remember all their wickedness: now their own doings have beset them about; they are before my face. They make the king glad with their wickedness, and the princes with their lies. They *are* all adulterers, as an oven heated by the baker, *who* ceaseth from raising after he hath kneaded the dough, until it be leavened. In the day of our king the princes have made *him* sick with bottles of wine; he stretched out his hand with scorners. For they have made ready their heart like an oven, whiles they lie in wait: their baker sleepeth all the night; in the morning it burneth as a flaming fire. They are all hot as an oven, and have devoured their judges; all their kings are fallen: *there is* none among them that calleth unto me. Ephraim, he hath mixed himself among the people; Ephraim is a cake not turned. Strangers have devoured his strength, and he knoweth *it* not: yea, gray hairs are here and there upon him, yet he knoweth not. And the pride of Israel testifieth to his face: and they do not return to the LORD their God, nor seek him for all this. Ephraim also is like a silly dove without heart: they call to Egypt, they go to Assyria. When they shall go, I will spread my net upon them; I will bring them down as the fowls of the heaven; I will chastise them, as their congregation hath heard. Woe unto them! for they have fled from me: destruction unto them! because they have transgressed against me: though I have redeemed them, yet they have spoken lies against me. And they have not cried unto me with their heart, when they howled upon their beds: they assemble themselves for corn and wine, *and* they rebel against me. Though I have bound *and* strengthened their arms, yet do they imagine mischief against me. They return, *but* not to the most High: they are like a deceitful bow: their princes shall fall by the sword for the rage of their tongue: this *shall be* their derision in the land of Egypt."

God's intention for Israel was that they should be a powerful nation, mightily blessed of God. Instead, they had allowed strangers to so rob them of their strength that they had become weak and dependent upon godless nations for support. There were among them the telling evidences of a dying nation. Gray hairs were sprinkled here and there upon the nation's head. They are described as a nation of drunkards and evil doers blinded to truth and zealous for evil. Their hearts were so full of evil desires that God describes them as being like an overheated oven. Their lives were fully controlled by selfish, sinful passions that blazed like a raging fire. They were like an unturned pancake- burned on one side, raw on the other. The good which they pretended was wholly spoiled by the evil to which they were fully devoted. They were obnoxious and odious to holy God.

Israel was in a condition of decay. They were moving swiftly toward death. This condition was evidenced by the strangers with whom they mingled and the gray hairs that were upon them.

The question that I would like to bring before our hearts today is this- Are there strangers and gray hairs in our lives? Strangers represent that which is contrary to God. Gray hairs are evidence of waning strength and impending death. Let us center our attention upon verse 9:

Ho 7:9 "Strangers have devoured his strength, and he knoweth *it* not: yea, gray hairs are here and there upon him, yet he knoweth not."

The Strangers

The word "strangers" refers to foreigners. They were non-Jewish people with whom Ephraim (Israel) had mingled. They were "uncircumcised," that is, they were not consecrated to God. They were idolaters, and Israel had not only mixed with them; they had adopted their ways and bowed to their gods.

The Strangers Spiritually Represented:

The "strangers" of Hosea 1 signify a rebellious and disobedient heart. Israel was to be a separate nation totally devoted to God. They were not to mingle with the idolatrous and sinful nations about them. Israel was to be a holy people given up to God and His will, but these strangers had turned their heart from God and had polluted their lives with evil practices.

This is the same situation for believers today. God has called us to love Him above all:

De 6:5 "And thou shalt love the LORD thy God with all thine heart, and with all thy soul, and with all thy might."

Mt 22:37-38 "Jesus said unto him, Thou shalt love the Lord thy God with all thy heart, and with all thy soul, and with all thy mind. This is the first and great commandment."

As believers, Jesus Christ is to be our Master. This lack of separation and love of the world- our lust for possessions, our self-seeking, our covetousness –often lead Christians to make unholy alliances with the world:

1Jo 2:15-17 "Love not the world, neither the things *that are* in the world. If any man love the world, the love of the Father is not in him. For all that *is* in the world, the lust of the flesh, and the lust of the eyes, and the pride of life, is not of the Father, but is of the world. And the world passeth away, and the lust thereof: but he that doeth the will of God abideth for ever."

These strangers may be symbolic of anything which dampens or dims our love for God and commitment to God.

The Unturned Cake:

Are we, like Israel, as an unturned pancake in God's eyes? Overcooked and burned because of our lust for the material things of this world- because we give more time and dedication to the things that are temporal than to the things of God? Yet, are we uncooked on the other side as far as our relationship to God?

The raw side pictures an unattended relationship with God- when we have no time for the Word of God or prayer, no time for service to God, or for attendance at church, then we are raw toward our God. When we have no interest in the things of God- when our worship of God becomes just a matter of convenience or routine, we are like that raw, unturned cake. Is our worship of God something we do out of love for Him because we desire to draw close to Him? Or is it is just an empty exercise we go through out of habit?

The Deceitful Bows:

Ho 7:16 "They return, *but* not to the most High: they are like a deceitful bow: their princes shall fall by the sword for the rage of their tongue: this *shall be* their derision in the land of Egypt."

Are we like deceitful bows- undependable and untrustworthy; going away from the living God rather than drawing near to Him? Are we living for the wrong purposes?

The "strangers" speak of any worldly or selfish attitude which may be controlling our lives: pride, self-exaltation, immorality, lust, covetousness, envy, bitterness, hate, unforgiveness, unkindness, indifference to others and to God, criticism, evil-speaking, a judgmental spirit, etc.

The Strangers Are Foreign Invaders:

These invading sins are contrary to God and His character. They rob us of our first love for God and our likeness to Christ. It is God's plan to fill us with Himself and produce in us Christ-likeness:

Ro 12:2 "And be not conformed to this world: but be ye transformed by the renewing of your mind, that ye may prove what *is* that good, and acceptable, and perfect, will of God."

Satan's greatest purpose for the Christian is to keep us from knowing God in His transforming power. Have we allowed "strangers" to invade our lives to keep us from experiencing God's power? Is there Christlikeness in my will, in my relationships, in my obedience, in my service, in my faith, and in my prayer life? Or, is there evidence of death and decay in my spiritual life?

The Gray Hairs:

The gray hairs of the nation of Israel are indicative of waning strength and impending death. Physically, gray hairs signify the fact that we are growing old and dying. They are the result of Adam's sin:

Ro 5:12 "Wherefore, as by one man sin entered into the world, and death by sin; and so death passed upon all men, for that all have sinned:"

Spiritually, the gray hairs picture decline in our relationship with God because we have allowed the "strangers" of sin and the world to invade our lives. The gray hairs for Israel were a clear indicator of their waning strength in God's sight. Hosea was telling the nation that there were signs everywhere that they were a dying nation.

Is that true also of America? Is that true of our church? Is it true of my life personally? How does God see us?

Gray Hairs are Indicative of a Serious Spiritual Problem:

The Bible clearly declares the awful consequences of sin in the life of the believer as well as that of the unbeliever:

Ro 6:23 "For the wages of sin *is* death; but the gift of God *is* eternal life through Jesus Christ our Lord."

Ro 8:12-13 "Therefore, brethren, we are debtors, not to the flesh, to live after the flesh. For if ye live after the flesh, ye shall die: but if ye through the Spirit do mortify the deeds of the body, ye shall live."

Ga 6:7-8 "Be not deceived; God is not mocked: for whatsoever a man soweth, that shall he also reap. For he that soweth to his flesh shall of the flesh reap corruption; but he that soweth to the Spirit shall of the Spirit reap life everlasting."

Gray hairs come about naturally. They require no effort. Spiritual gray hairs come about because of no effort to prevent them. They come because of a failure to yield to God and to walk in the Spirit's strength. They are the fruit of yielding to the flesh and the world. They are often unobserved at first.

These Gray Hairs are Identifiable:

They are identified by a diminished sense of God's presence in our lives.

They are identified by a lessened sense of the awfulness of sin:

How we see this in our nation and throughout our society today! There is rampant immorality, perversion, lying, crookedness, abortion, and every vice. Yet, there is so little concern among the lost or among God's own people.

There is a waning interest in and commitment to the things of God such as Bible study, prayer, or soul winning.

There is a loss of peace, and a lack of gratitude, joy, and praise to God.

There is powerlessness in the work of God.

There is fruitlessness, cowardice, and timidity.

There is no concern for the lost.

There is hardness of heart and stubborn pride:

We see this in our text in verse 7:

Ho 7:10 "And the pride of Israel testifieth to his face: and they do not return to the LORD their God, nor seek him for all this."

So, what are we to do? We see next:

<u>The Remedy</u>

Ho 7:13-16 "Woe unto them! for they have fled from me: destruction unto them! because they have transgressed against me: though I have redeemed them, yet they have spoken lies against me. And they have not cried unto me with their heart, when they howled upon their beds: they assemble themselves for corn and wine, *and* they rebel against me. Though I have bound *and* strengthened their arms, yet do they imagine mischief against me. They return, *but* not to the most High: they are like a deceitful bow: their princes shall fall by the sword for the rage of their tongue: this *shall be* their derision in the land of Egypt."

We find the remedy in doing the **opposite** of what Israel had done:

They had Lied:

If we are to escape the effects of the strangers and gray hairs in our spiritual lives, we must be willing to face the truth of our condition. We must be honest with God and repent:

Isa 1:18 "Come now, and let us reason together, saith the LORD: though your sins be as scarlet, they shall be as white as snow; though they be red like crimson, they shall be as wool."

They had not cried to God:

If we want to have God's blessing and power again, we must cry out to Him with an earnest desire to be right with Him. Jesus said,

Re 3:19-20 "As many as I love, I rebuke and chasten: be zealous therefore, and repent. Behold, I stand at the door, and knock: if any man hear my voice, and open the door, I will come in to him, and will sup with him, and he with me."

They Blamed God for their Problems Rather than Repenting of their Sins:

We must take responsibility for our condition. If we are not living in power and victory, it is not God's fault. He has given us all we need in Christ.

They Refused to Return to God in Sincerity and Truth:

This is what is required if we would escape the chastisement and judgment of God. Israel turned away from the LORD, and the result was awful judgment:

Ho 7:16 "...their princes shall fall by the sword for the rage of their tongue: this *shall be* their derision in the land of Egypt."

To Live is Christ

This is always true. Sin always bears bad fruit and brings serious consequences.

There is but One Remedy for the Strangers and Gray Hairs in the Life of a Christian:

-The strangers- the lusts of the eyes, the hidden sins, the love of this world, the indifference, etc. -must be removed through repentance.

-The gray hairs must be seen as a symptom of spiritual death and revival and restoration urgently sought.

-When the strangers are removed by true repentance and surrender, the gray hairs will disappear.

-God's Holy Spirit is the source of power and victory.

The key to spiritual power and fruitfulness is to repent of sin and surrender to the full power of the Holy Spirit of God.

"Lord, I'm Coming Home"

I've wandered far away from God,

Now I'm coming home;

The paths of sin too long I've trod,

Lord, I'm coming home.

Refrain:

Coming home, coming home,

Nevermore to roam;

Open wide Thine arms of love,

Lord, I'm coming home.

I've wasted many precious years,

Now I'm coming home;

I now repent with bitter tears,

Lord, I'm coming home.

I'm tired of sin and straying, Lord,

Now I'm coming home;

I'll trust Thy love, believe Thy word,

Lord, I'm coming home.

My soul is sick, my heart is sore,

Now I'm coming home;

My strength renew, my hope restore,

Lord, I'm coming home.

My only hope, my only plea,

Now I'm coming home;

That Jesus died, and died for me,

Lord, I'm coming home.

I need His cleansing blood I know,

Now I'm coming home;

Oh, wash me whiter than the snow,

Lord, I'm coming home.

Refrain:

Coming home, coming home,

Nevermore to roam;

Open wide Thine arms of love,

Lord, I'm coming home.

- William J. Kirkpatrick, pub.1892

Chapter 14

"What Time Is It?"

Ro 13:11-14 "And that, knowing the time, that now *it is* high time to awake out of sleep: for now *is* our salvation nearer than when we believed. The night is far spent, the day is at hand: let us therefore cast off the works of darkness, and let us put on the armour of light. Let us walk honestly, as in the day; not in rioting and drunkenness, not in chambering and wantonness, not in strife and envying. But put ye on the Lord Jesus Christ, and make not provision for the flesh, to *fulfil* the lusts *thereof*."

A reporter once asked a passerby, "Do you know what the two greatest problems in America are?" The pedestrian responded, "I don't know, and I don't care!" The reporter exclaimed, "Then you've got both of them!" This man was both ignorant and apathetic.

God addresses both of these problems in the passage we just read, and He urges us to take due consideration of the time. Do you know the time? God tells us that "the night is far spent, the day is at hand." We need to consider the time. What time is it? God answers this question in four points:

<u>It is Time to Wake Up:</u>

It is Time to Wake up to the Perilous Times Around Us:

We are living in the time when the "night is far spent." We are living in the black night of humanity and the perilous times predicted in the Scriptures:

2Ti 3:1-5 "This know also, that in the last days perilous times shall come. For men shall be lovers of their own selves, covetous, boasters, proud, blasphemers, disobedient to parents, unthankful, unholy, Without natural affection, trucebreakers, false accusers, incontinent, fierce, despisers of those that are good,

Traitors, heady, highminded, lovers of pleasures more than lovers of God; Having a form of godliness, but denying the power thereof: from such turn away."

We are living in times when the foundations are being destroyed- in days foreshadowed by the days of Noah -days that Jesus said would be characteristic of the time of His coming:

Ge 6:5 "And GOD saw that the wickedness of man *was* great in the earth, and *that* every imagination of the thoughts of his heart *was* only evil continually."

Mt 24:37 "But as the days of Noe *were*, so shall also the coming of the Son of man be."

We are living in days when there are no moral absolutes. Days like the times of the judges of Israel, when "every man did *that which was* right in his own eyes."

The passage in 2 Timothy 3 surely describes our day- when self is the first love, when pleasure is more important than God- television, sports, entertainment, and possessions are valued above God.

We are living in times when parents are murdering their own unborn babies, when children are killing other children, when parents abuse and molest their children, when children even kill their own parents, and every perversion is permitted and celebrated- when people are "without natural affection," and are fierce "despisers of those that are good."

Read it again:

2Ti 3:2-4 "For men shall be lovers of their own selves, covetous, boasters, proud, blasphemers, disobedient to parents, unthankful, unholy, Without natural affection, trucebreakers, false accusers, incontinent, fierce, despisers of those that are good, Traitors, heady, highminded, lovers of pleasures more than lovers of God."

So, we see that we are living in the night.

But here God also speaks of the "day" that is at hand. That day is a reminder again of that glorious day when Jesus Christ comes again. The question is, Are we awake? Are we prepared? Are we aware of the perilous times in which we live? Do we love His appearing? It's time to wake up to the time.

<u>It it Time to Look Up:</u>

It is time to look up to the prospect of Jesus Christ's soon return:

Paul says that we need to look up, "for now is our salvation nearer than when we believed." That same Jesus who was laid as a babe in a manger, who made God known through His person and power, and who died for our sins and rose again, who came once in humility, is coming again in power and great glory!

The time of His coming is not known by any but God:

Mr 13:32-33 "But of that day and *that* hour knoweth no man, no, not the angels which are in heaven, neither the Son, but the Father. Take ye heed, watch and pray: for ye know not when the time is."

Christ's coming will be in two stages:

<u>He is coming first in the air for the Church:</u>

Th 4:16-17 "For the Lord himself shall descend from heaven with a shout, with the voice of the archangel, and with the trump of God: and the dead in Christ shall rise first: Then we which are alive *and* remain shall be caught up together with them in the clouds, to meet the Lord in the air: and so shall we ever be with the Lord."

That coming will be sudden and unexpected, like a thief in the night. It could happen at any moment. Those without Christ will be left behind. Many of the unsaved scoff at Christ's coming just as the Bible said they would:

2Pe 3:3-4 "Knowing this first, that there shall come in the last days scoffers, walking after their own lusts, And saying, Where is the promise of his coming..."

Others are indifferent to Christ's return. But Jesus' return is sure. It will be sudden as He said,

Re 22:7 "Behold, I come quickly: blessed *is* he that keepeth the sayings of the prophecy of this book."

For the believer, the coming of Jesus Christ is the blessed hope that should motivate us to live soberly and righteously in this present world:

Tit 2:12-13 "Teaching us that, denying ungodliness and worldly lusts, we should live soberly, righteously, and godly, in this present world; Looking for that blessed hope, and the glorious appearing of the great God and our Saviour Jesus Christ;"

We must live in the reality of this blessed hope, when the former things will pass away, and all things will be made new. What a day that will be!

In the second phase of His coming Jesus will return to the earth in power and great glory to judge the world:

Re 19:11-13 "And I saw heaven opened, and behold a white horse; and he that sat upon him *was* called Faithful and True, and in righteousness he doth judge and make war. His eyes *were* as a flame of fire, and on his head *were* many crowns; and he had a name written, that no man knew, but he himself. And he *was* clothed with a vesture dipped in blood: and his name is called The Word of God."

And so, in the light of Christ's sure return,

It is Time to Clean Up:

Ro 13:12, 13, 14 "...let us therefore cast off the works of darkness...Let us walk honestly, as in the day; not in rioting and drunkenness, not in chambering and wantonness, not in strife and envying... and make not provision for the flesh, to *fulfil* the lusts *thereof*."

For the Christian, this means we are to cast off the works of the night. We live in a day of compromise and no absolutes, but the Christian is not to live like that. We are to call sin "sin," and cast it from us. We are to get the works of darkness out of our lives and cast them out like a filthy garment. We need to realize that sin in our lives is of the devil. It is an offense to our God. We are not to live in "wantonness," which means just doing what we feel like doing; we are to live in obedience to God and His Word. Sin must be faced in the life of a Christian, and then confessed, forgiven, and forsaken! God wants us to get rid of every selfish and lustful desire. We need to cast it off! Paul is addressing Christians in this passage. He is telling them it's time to clean up!

For the lost, it's time to turn to Jesus Christ and be saved before it is too late. You may think you can clean up your act and turn over a new leaf, but you will go to hell. You need a new heart. You need to be born again! God is the One who will help you clean up your life.

<u>It's Time to Dress Up</u>

The Armor of Light:

Ro 13:12, 14 "...and let us put on the armour of light..."But put ye on the Lord Jesus Christ..."

After we cast off the sin, it's time to dress up in God's armor of light. This armor is clearly identified in Ephesians 6:

Eph 6:13-18 "Wherefore take unto you the whole armour of God, that ye may be able to withstand in the evil day, and having done all, to stand. Stand therefore, having your loins girt about with truth, and having on the breastplate of righteousness; And your feet shod with the preparation of the gospel of peace; Above all, taking the shield of faith, wherewith ye shall be able to quench all the fiery darts of the wicked. And take the helmet of salvation, and the sword of the Spirit, which is the word of God: Praying always with all prayer and supplication in the Spirit, and watching thereunto with all perseverance and supplication for all saints;"

To Live is Christ

The Girdle of Truth speaks of a life guided and governed by obedience to God's Word.

The Breastplate of Righteousness is a life fully committed to righteous living.

The Shoes of Gospel Readiness is a life ready to witness and serve.

The Shield of Faith is a life of faith- ready to live in full dependence upon God.

The Helmet of Salvation is a life assured of salvation through faith in Christ.

The Sword of the Spirit is a life prepared through study, meditation, and memorization of God's Word. It is a life ready to fight Satan and live in victory over sin and for God's cause.

The Prayerful Admonition speaks of a life given to prayer.

We Need to Dress Ourselves In Christ Jesus Our Lord:

Ro 13:14 "But put ye on the Lord Jesus Christ..."

If we are saved, the Bible declares that we are in Christ. This phrase, "in Christ" is used many times in the New Testament. As Christians, we must know and yield to what and who we are in Christ Jesus our Lord.

We are:

New creatures in Christ

Crucified with Christ

Dead to sin

Alive unto God

Free from condemnation

Accepted in the beloved

Indwelt by God's Spirit

Witnesses for Christ

We must put on the Lord Jesus Christ and live as ambassadors for our Heavenly King by waking up to the times we live in, putting off the works of darkness, and putting on Jesus Christ in a life of faith and surrender to Him.

What time is it? It is time to wake up, it is time to look up, it is time to clean up, and it is time to dress up.

"Take My Life and Let It Be"

Take my life and let it be

Consecrated, Lord, to Thee.

Take my moments and my days,

Let them flow in ceaseless praise.

Take my hands and let them move

At the impulse of Thy love.

Take my feet and let them be

Swift and beautiful for Thee.

Take my voice and let me sing,

Always, only for my King.

Take my lips and let them be

Filled with messages from Thee.

Take my silver and my gold,

Not a mite would I withhold.

Take my intellect and use

Every pow'r as Thou shalt choose.

Take my will and make it Thine,

It shall be no longer mine.

Take my heart, it is Thine own,

It shall be Thy royal throne.

Take my love, my Lord, I pour

At Thy feet its treasure store.

Take myself and I will be

Ever, only, all for Thee.

-Frances R. Havergal, 1874

Chapter 15

"What Christmas Means to Me"
(Preached December 24, 1989)

Lu 2:1-20 "And it came to pass in those days, that there went out a decree from Caesar Augustus, that all the world should be taxed. (*And* this taxing was first made when Cyrenius was governor of Syria.) And all went to be taxed, every one into his own city. And Joseph also went up from Galilee, out of the city of Nazareth, into Judaea, unto the city of David, which is called Bethlehem; (because he was of the house and lineage of David:) To be taxed with Mary his espoused wife, being great with child. And so it was, that, while they were there, the days were accomplished that she should be delivered. And she brought forth her firstborn son, and wrapped him in swaddling clothes, and laid him in a manger; because there was no room for them in the inn. And there were in the same country shepherds abiding in the field, keeping watch over their flock by night. And, lo, the angel of the Lord came upon them, and the glory of the Lord shone round about them: and they were sore afraid. And the angel said unto them, Fear not: for, behold, I bring you good tidings of great joy, which shall be to all people. For unto you is born this day in the city of David a Saviour, which is Christ the Lord. And this *shall be* a sign unto you; Ye shall find the babe wrapped in swaddling clothes, lying in a manger. And suddenly there was with the angel a multitude of the heavenly host praising God, and saying, Glory to God in the highest, and on earth peace, good will toward men. And it came to pass, as the angels were gone away from them into heaven, the shepherds said one to another, Let us now go even unto Bethlehem, and see this thing which is come to pass, which the Lord hath made known unto us. And they came with haste, and found Mary, and Joseph, and the babe lying in a manger. And when they had seen *it*, they made known abroad the saying which was told them concerning this child. And all they that heard *it* wondered at those things which were told them by the shepherds. But Mary kept all these things, and pondered *them* in her heart. And the shepherds returned, glorifying and praising God for all the things that they had heard and seen, as it was told unto them."

To Live is Christ

What does Christmas mean to me?

Christmas Means That God Can Be Trusted

Christmas Means that God has kept His Word:

God sent the promised One:

To be born in Bethlehem-

Mic 5:2 "But thou, Bethlehem Ephratah, *though* thou be little among the thousands of Judah, *yet* out of thee shall he come forth unto me *that is* to be ruler in Israel; whose goings forth *have been* from of old, from everlasting."

To be born of a virgin:

Isa 7:14 "Therefore the Lord himself shall give you a sign; Behold, a virgin shall conceive, and bear a son, and shall call his name Immanuel."

To grow up as a tender plant:

Isa 53:1-2 "Who hath believed our report? and to whom is the arm of the LORD revealed? For he shall grow up before him as a tender plant, and as a root out of a dry ground:"

To be a prophet, like unto Moses:

De 18:15 "The LORD thy God will raise up unto thee a Prophet from the midst of thee, of thy brethren, like unto me; unto him ye shall hearken;"

To be wounded for our transgressions and bruised for our iniquities:

Isa 53:5 "But he *was* wounded for our transgressions, *he was* bruised for our iniquities: the chastisement of our peace *was* upon him; and with his stripes we are healed."

To bruise the serpent's head:

Ge 3:15 "And I will put enmity between thee and the woman, and between thy seed and her seed; it shall bruise thy head, and thou shalt bruise his heel."

Christmas Means that God has Demonstrated His Love:

The Babe whom Mary wrapped in swaddling clothes and laid in a manger was God's love gift to the world:

Joh 3:16 "For God so loved the world, that he gave his only begotten Son, that whosoever believeth in him should not perish, but have everlasting life."

1Jo 4:14 "And we have seen and do testify that the Father sent the Son *to be* the Saviour of the world."

Nothing could better demonstrate God's selfless love than the sending of His own Son to be our Savior. What greater evidence could we have of God's sincerity and fidelity?

Ro 5:8 "But God commendeth his love toward us, in that, while we were yet sinners, Christ died for us."

Christmas Means that God is the Great Giver

God's giving of His Son revealed His heart, for God is love:

1Jo 4:8-10 "He that loveth not knoweth not God; for God is love. In this was manifested the love of God toward us, because that God sent his only begotten Son into the world, that we might live through him. Herein is love, not that we loved God, but that he loved us, and sent his Son *to be* the propitiation for our sins."

The nature of love is to give. God is not a taker. He desires our love and obedience only that He might give more of Himself to us. He desires our faith only that He might bless us more fully. He desires our gifts only that He may enrich us more fully.

It is an amazing truth that God's desire is to share His power and glory with a fallen race. In light of His mercy and gifts to us, it is foolish for us to withhold anything of ourselves from God who gave so much for us:

Ro 12:1 "I beseech you therefore, brethren, by the mercies of God, that ye present your bodies a living sacrifice, holy, acceptable unto God, *which is* your reasonable service."

God's intent is to enrich us for all eternity:

Ro 6:23 "...the gift of God *is* eternal life through Jesus Christ our Lord."

Christmas Means that God Knows How I Feel:

Because Jesus Christ left the glories of Heaven to come to earth in human flesh, He has experienced life in a human body. He was a baby. He became a child. He grew to be a teenager. He grew to manhood; and He died.

Jesus lived a common life. He was a human being. He faced temptation. He studied, learned, grew, obeyed, worked, ate, and slept:

Lu 2:51-52 "And he went down with them, and came to Nazareth, and was subject unto them: but his mother kept all these sayings in her heart. And Jesus increased in wisdom and stature, and in favour with God and man."

Mt 4:1-2 "Then was Jesus led up of the Spirit into the wilderness to be tempted of the devil. And when he had fasted forty days and forty nights, he was afterward an hungred."

Jesus experienced human frailty and weakness in His physical body. He was hungry. He grew weary. The Bible says that He was tempted in every point just as we are, yet without sin:

Heb 4:15 "For we have not an high priest which cannot be touched with the feeling of our infirmities; but was in all points tempted like as *we are, yet* without sin."

Jesus, in His humanity, was ordinary. He was no superman:

Isa 53:1-3 "Who hath believed our report? and to whom is the arm of the LORD revealed? For he shall grow up before him as a tender plant, and as a root out of a dry ground: he hath no form nor comeliness; and when we shall see him, *there is* no beauty that we should desire him. He is despised and rejected of men; a man of sorrows, and acquainted with grief: and we hid as it were *our* faces from him; he was despised, and we esteemed him not."

He experienced human feelings- love, compassion, loneliness, sorrow and weeping:

Joh 11:34-36 "And said, Where have ye laid him? They said unto him, Lord, come and see. Jesus wept. Then said the Jews, Behold how he loved him!"

Mt 26:38 "Then saith he unto them, My soul is exceeding sorrowful, even unto death: tarry ye here, and watch with me."

Because Jesus came, He understands our feelings and infirmities.

Christmas Means That I Can Know God and Enjoy His Fellowship Forever

Christmas Means Revelation- God Became Man:

Joh 1:14 "And the Word was made flesh, and dwelt among us, (and we beheld his glory, the glory as of the only begotten of the Father,) full of grace and truth."

The Word, Jesus Christ, has been made flesh. God has come in flesh to declare Himself to mankind. Light has shined into our darkness:

Joh 1:9-12 "*That* was the true Light, which lighteth every man that cometh into the world. He was in the world, and the world was made by him, and the world knew him not. He came unto his own, and his own received him not. But as many as received him, to them gave he power to become the sons of God, *even* to them that believe on his name:"

To Live is Christ

The infinite, Almighty, Eternal God has made Himself knowable to fallen humanity.

Christmas Means Salvation:

Because Jesus came, sinners can now be reconciled to God. The price of redemption was paid by the Son of God. Eternal life was provided through the gift of God's Son:

Col 1:19-21 "For it pleased *the Father* that in him should all fulness dwell; And, having made peace through the blood of his cross, by him to reconcile all things unto himself; by him, *I say*, whether *they be* things in earth, or things in heaven. And you, that were sometime alienated and enemies in *your* mind by wicked works, yet now hath he reconciled."

Christmas Means Fellowship:

Because Jesus came, we now have the gift of God's Spirit. We have fellowship with God through the Spirit and because of the Lord Jesus Christ:

1Jo 1:2-4 "(For the life was manifested, and we have seen *it*, and bear witness, and shew unto you that eternal life, which was with the Father, and was manifested unto us;) That which we have seen and heard declare we unto you, that ye also may have fellowship with us: and truly our fellowship *is* with the Father, and with his Son Jesus Christ. And these things write we unto you, that your joy may be full."

1Jo 1:7 "But if we walk in the light, as he is in the light, we have fellowship one with another, and the blood of Jesus Christ his Son cleanseth us from all sin."

Because Jesus came, we have access to the Father in prayer:

Eph 2:18 "For through him we both have access by one Spirit unto the Father."

Heb 4:16 "Let us therefore come boldly unto the throne of grace, that we may obtain mercy, and find grace to help in time of need."

Ro 8:15 "For ye have not received the spirit of bondage again to fear; but ye have received the Spirit of adoption, whereby we cry, Abba, Father."

Because Jesus came, we have forgiveness of sins:

Eph 1:7 "In whom we have redemption through his blood, the forgiveness of sins, according to the riches of his grace;"

Because Jesus came, we have an entrance into Heaven:

Joh 14:2-3 "In my Father's house are many mansions: if *it were* not *so*, I would have told you. I go to prepare a place for you. And if I go and prepare a place for you, I will come again, and receive you unto myself; that where I am, *there* ye may be also."

Christmas Means that I Belong to God

Because Jesus came and I have received Him, I belong to God. Christmas means that my life is not my own. It is God's to do with as He wills. I cannot deny Him the love that He deserves. I cannot refuse Him the trust that He encourages. I cannot withhold from Him the service that He enlists. I cannot despise the fellowship He offers. My life, body and soul, belong to Him who loved me and gave Himself for me:

Ga 2:20 "I am crucified with Christ: nevertheless I live; yet not I, but Christ liveth in me: and the life which I now live in the flesh I live by the faith of the Son of God, who loved me, and gave himself for me."

1Co 6:19 -20 "What? know ye not that your body is the temple of the Holy Ghost *which is* in you, which ye have of God, and ye are not your own? For ye are bought with a price: therefore glorify God in your body, and in your spirit, which are God's."

Php 2:5-7 Let this mind be in you, which was also in Christ Jesus: Who, being in the form of God, thought it not robbery to be equal with God: But made himself of no reputation, and took upon him the form of a servant, and was made in the

To Live is Christ

likeness of men: And being found in fashion as a man, he humbled himself, and became obedient unto death, even the death of the cross."

Christmas means all that Jesus Christ is to me!

"Down From His Glory"

Down from His glory,

Ever living story,

My God and Savior came,

And Jesus was His Name;

Born in a manger,

To His own a stranger,

A Man of sorrows, tears and agony.

Oh, how I love Him! How I adore Him!

My breath, my sunshine, my all in all;

The great Creator became my Savior,

And all God's fullness dwelleth in Him.

What condescension,

Bringing us redemption;

That in the dead of night,

Not one faint hope in sight,

God, gracious, tender,

Laid aside His splendor,

Stooping to woo, to win, to save my soul.

Oh, how I love Him! How I adore Him!

My breath, my sunshine, my all in all;

The great Creator became my Savior,

And all God's fullness dwelleth in Him.

Without reluctance,

Flesh and blood His substance,

He took the form of man,

Revealed the hidden plan,

Oh, glorious myst'ry,

Sacrifice of Calv'ry,

And now I know Thou art the great "I Am."

Oh, how I love Him! How I adore Him!

My breath, my sunshine, my all in all;

The great Creator became my Savior,

And all God's fullness dwelleth in Him.

-William E. Booth-Clibborn, 1921

Pictures and Memories:

Young Charles Howard Davis

Charles Howard Davis and Linda Faye Burdett

December 25, 1961, Hickory Grove Baptist Church

Huntland, Tennessee

Charles' Parents, Homer and Minnie Lou Davis

Linda's Parents, T.Z. and Sibyl Burdett

Charles and Linda with their three daughters- Krista Carol, Evangeline Faith,

And Aimee Charlene Davis

Linda and girls in Paducah, Kentucky where Charles

Pastored West End Baptist Church

Pastor Charles H. Davis, Wall Highway Baptist Church, Madison, Alabama

Breaking Ground for New Educational Building, Wall Highway Baptist Church

Charles and Linda while serving at First Baptist Church,

Grayson, Kentucky

Charles with his sister and brother,

Wanda Davis Fanning and Ray Davis

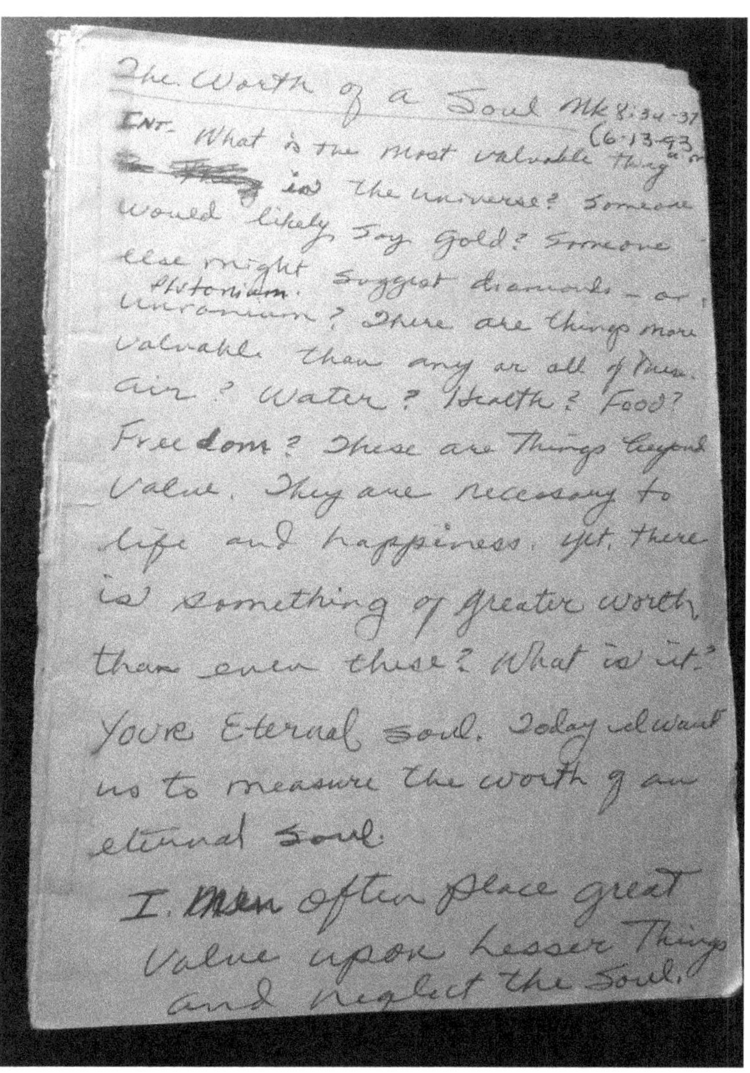

Example of Pastor Davis' Handwritten Sermon Notes

Certificate of Ordination

We, the undersigned, hereby certify that upon the recommendation and request of the _Donaldson Grove Baptist_ Church at _Rt. # 1 — Elora, Tennessee_ which had full and sufficient opportunity for judging his gifts, and after satisfactory examination by us in regard to his Christian experience, call to the ministry, and views of Bible doctrine,

Rev. Charles Howard Davis

was solemnly and publicly set apart and ordained to the work of

THE GOSPEL MINISTRY

by authority and order

of the _Donaldson Grove Baptist_ Church at _Rt. # 1 - Elora, Tennessee_ on the _6th_ day of _September_, 19_59_

ORDAINING COUNCIL

Rev. Howard McGehee
Moderator of Ordaining Council

Abe Silliman
Clerk of Ordaining Council

O. O. Bishop

R. B. Kennedy

B. L. Cantrell

E. J. Orr

Homer Orr

J. C. Stovall

REACH NEW HEIGHTS IN CHRISTIAN LIVING AND SERVICE!

Attend Sunday School And Church Every Sunday And

"Go Forward With The Lord"

Churchwide Attendance Campaign

February 8th Through March 15th

Sunday School	9:30 A.M.
Morning Worship	10:45 A.M.
Training Union	6:00 P.M.
Evening Worship	7:00 P.M.
Wednesday Prayer Service	7:15 P.M.

We invite you to make that "Special Effort" to attend all services during the "Forward For The Lord" Campaign. Help us to reach new heights for Christ. Come, be a part of that forward movement.

Sunday Feb. 8th Is The First Big Day. Don't Miss The Blessing Of Being "One Of Those Who Will Be Going Forward For The Lord."

Classes For All Ages Nursery Open For All Services.

WEST END BAPTIST CHURCH

324 SOUTH 28th STREET

"I press toward the mark of the high calling of God in Christ Jesus." ... Phil. 3:14

Feb 6 1970

Attend Every Service

CHRISTIAN LIFE CONFERENCE

March 15th through 19th

Two Outstanding Bible Preachers:

Bro. Billy B. Cooper
First Baptist Church
Carrollton, Ohio

Bro. James E. Rolison
First Baptist Church
Ardmore, Alabama

With Bible messages which will speak to your needs. God's way to true happiness, peace and a spirit filled life. Bible answers to problems you face! Find your way to Christian victory and holiness.

Attendance Goal Sunday 347–Help Us Reach It!

SPECIAL SERVICES SUNDAY

9:30 a.m. Special Bible Study by the Pastor for Youth I through Adults in Auditorium. Regular Sunday School for Nursery through Juniors.

10:45 a.m. Worship hour with Guest Speaker Bro. Billy B. Cooper.

6:00 p.m. Bible Study by the Pastor in Auditorium for Youth I through Adults. Regular Training Union for Nursery through Junior ages.

7:00 p.m. Worship hour with Guest Speaker Bro. Billy B. Cooper.

SERVICES MON. through THURS.

6:30 p.m. Bible Study in Romans by Bro. Charles Davis.

7:00 p.m. Bible Message by Bro. James E. Rolison.

7:45 p.m. Bible Message by Bro. Billy B. Cooper.

Nursery For All Services

WEST END BAPTIST CHURCH

28th and Clark Streets

Paved Off Street Parking

LAST WEEK'S REPORT
    Sunday School Attendance   67
    Church Training   40
    Total Offering   569.08
OPPORTUNITIES OF SERVICE FOR THE WEEK
    TODAY
        H O M E C O M I N G
        Lunch at Recreational Building and Singing
        to follow - EVERYONE IS INVITED!!!
    TUESDAY
        7:30 p.m. - Asso. Ex. Board Mtg.-BSU
    MONDAY-SATURDAY
        W.M.U. Fair Booth - Maury County Fair
    WEDNESDAY
        7:30 p.m. - Prayer Service
    THURSDAY
        1:30-7:30 p.m.-Picture taking for Directory
    FRIDAY
        4:00-9:00 p.m. - Picture taking for Directory
ATTENTION
    If you plan to go bowling, please sign your
name on the list in the back. Cards are on the
table in front of the pulpit for you to fill out
and return the day that we go bowling.
W E L C O M E
    We are happy to welcome Bro. Charles Davis to
our service today! Bro. Davis is a former pastor
of Rock Springs. We pray God's richest blessings
on him today as he brings our morning message.
H O M E C O M I N G   T O D A Y !!!!

    Today is the 130th Anniversary of Rock Springs
Baptist Church. We will be having dinner at the
recreational building immediately following the
worship service. Then we will all come back to
the church for singing at 1:45 p.m. We have two
special groups of singers: the choir from Third
Baptist Church in Nashville and the Victory Leaders.
We hope you will make your plans to stay and enjoy
the fellowship throughout the day!
NO   WORSHIP   SERVICE TONIGHT!!!!

ATTENTION- Please sign your name on the schedule
in the back today if you haven't already done so,
to have your picture taken for our pictoral directory!
Someone will be back there to assist you if you need

Bro. Davis preaching at Rock Springs Baptist Church's Anniversary Service

REVIVAL
August 16 thru 21, 1976
7:30 Nightly
OAKLAWN BAPTIST CHURCH
Winchester, Tennessee
Evangelist
CHARLES DAVIS
WALL HIGHWAY BAPTIST CHURCH
NEAR HUNTSVILLE. ALA.
Singer
BILL FOWLER
FIRST BAPTIST CHURCH
FLINTVILLE. TN.
CHARLES DAVIS
RAY GARDNER, Pastor
Everyone Is Welcome

Madison Church Selects Davis As New Pastor

Charles H. Davis has been named pastor of the Wall Highway Baptist Church in Madison. A native of Huntland, Tenn.,

Davis led churches in Tennessee, Alabama, and Kentucky before resigning a Chicago, Ill. pastorate to accept the Wall Highway church. He is married to the former Linda Burdett and has three children, Krista, 12, Evangeline, 10 and Aimee, 5.

The Rev. Davis will preach his first Sunday sermon at the church August 31.

CHARLES DAVIS

Wall Highway Baptist Will Host Revival Nov. 30-Dec. 7

Revival services will be conducted at the Wall Highway Baptist Church of Rt. #2, Madison, Alabama, Nov. 30 through Dec. 7. Charles Davis, the pastor, will be the speaker for these services. The services will include the 11:00 a.m. and the 6:00 p.m. services on Sundays and special services each evening, Monday through Saturday at 7:00 p.m. The Church is located on the Wall-Triana Highway, one and one-half miles north of Highway 72. A nursery will be provided for all services. The public is cordially invited to attend.

high school in Gurley, Ala. Several groups will sing. Make plans to attend. Starting time is 7 pm.

Don't forget to send me your dates and comments for your singings.

Until next time, keep a happy heart.

WALL HIGHWAY CHURCH, HUNTSVILLE PLANS NEW EDUCATION BUILDING—

Wall Highway Church, Route 2, Madison, observed its twelfth anniversary July 31 with special services and a groundbreaking ceremony for a new 9,600 sq. ft. educational annex. Ray Walker, former pastor of the church, was guest speaker for the afternoon services and Charles Davis, pastor, brought the morning message. An all-time high attendance of 301 was present for Sunday School, with 180 of these riding the five buses operated by the church. Those in the picture are, left to right: Avery Grant, contractor; Bob Tidwell; Julian Pope, building committee chairman; Charles Davis, pastor; and Earl Maynard. Members of the building committee not pictured are Bill Olive and Jim Pitts.

WHEN GOD VISITS HIS PEOPLE IN A
MIGHTY WAY SOMETHING GOOD HAPPENS
TO US. WE CALL THIS REVIVAL. LET
US PRAY WITH ALL OF OUR MIGHT THAT
GOD WILL BE HERE THIS WEEK IN A MIGHTY
WAY. LET US EXPECT GOOD THINGS HAPPEN
TO US THIS WEEK.
 GOD HAS SENT ONE OF HIS FINEST SERVANTS
TO PREACH HIS WORD. BROTHER CHARLES
DAVIS IS GODS ANNOINTED MAN FOR THIS
MEETING.HE IS PASTOR OF WALL HIGHWAY
BAPTIST CHURCH. LAST YEAR THEY HAD 44
BAPTISMS AND 38 ADDITIONS BY LETTER.
 GOD WILL NOT WASTE THE PRECIOUS TIME
OF A MAN LIKE CHARLES DAVIS. CHARLES
WAS SENT TO PREACH THE WORD OF GOD. HE
IS GOD'S MAN OF THE WEEK HERE AT GALILEE.
 SINCE GOD HAS BLESSED US WITH SUCH A
MAN LET US THROW OUR SUPPORT BEHIND HIM
AND LET GOD REALLY TURN HIM LOOSE. I
KNOW THAT THIS CHURCH NEEDS AND WANTS
REVIVAL TO COME THIS WEEK.IT CAN REALLY
HAPPEN HERE THIS WEEK. GOD DOES ALL
THINGS WELL AND HE CAN AND WILL SEND
REVIVAL TO US HERE IN GALILEE BAPTIST
CHURCH.
 CHARLES MAY GOD BLESS AND USE YOU THIS
WEEK. I PERSONALLY BELIEVE THAT THIS WILL
BE AN UNUSUAL AND PROSPEROUS WEEK FOR
GALILEE BAPTIST CHURCH BECAUSE THAT YOU
ARE HERE. I AM LOOKING FORWARD TO WORKING
WITH YOU THIS WEEK.

                    ROLLAND LEE PASTOR.

Revival Annoucement, Galilee Baptist Church, 1978

REVIVAL SERVICES
MT. PLEASANT BAPTIST CHURCH
ACROSS FROM SUSAN MOORE SCHOOL
BETWEEN ONEONTA AND SNEAD, ONE MILE OFF HIGHWAY 75
MAY 6th - 13th, 1979
★ GREAT GOSPEL SINGING
★ ADULT AND YOUTH CHOIRS
★ SOLOS
★ CONGREGATIONAL SINGING
AT ITS BEST
MUSIC DIRECTOR: ROBERT KING
SPEAKER: CHARLES H. DAVIS
REVIVAL MESSAGES
Sunday, 11:00 a.m. "IS THIS THE LAST GENERATION?"
7:00 p.m. "WHO ARE JEHOVAH'S WITNESSES?"
Monday: 7:00 p.m. "ARE WE IN THE GREAT TRIBULATION?"
Tuesday: 7:00 p.m. "WHERE ARE THE DEAD?"
Wednesday: 7:00 p.m. "HEAVEN, WHERE IS IT, WHAT WILL IT
BE LIKE, AND WHO WILL BE THERE?"
Thursday, 7:00 p.m. "IS THERE A HELL?"
Friday, 7:00 p.m. "ONE JUDGEMENT OR FOUR?"
Saturday, 7:00 p.m. "ARMAGEDDON: WILL YOU BE THERE?"
Sunday, 11:00 a.m. "WILL THERE BE A MILLENIUM?"
7:00 p.m. "WHAT TO DO UNTIL JESUS COMES."

Rev. Charles Davis

First Baptist Calls Pastor

The First Baptist Church, Court St., Grayson, has called a new pastor, Rev. Charles Davis.

Davis has been on the church field since Nov. 21. He comes to Grayson from the Unity Baptist Church in Ashland.

A dinner was held Nov. 19 at the church in honor of Rev. Davis, to welcome he and his family to the church. He and his wife, Linda, have three daughters, Krista, Vangy and Aimee.

Members of the church and Rev. Davis invite the public to attend services: Sunday School, 9:30 a.m.; morning worship, 10:45 a.m.; evening worship; 7 p.m. and Wednesday night prayer service, 7 p.m.

Charles Davis,
Evangelist

183

185

www.ingramcontent.com/pod-product-compliance
Lightning Source LLC
Chambersburg PA
CBHW052001150726
47999CB00004B/1476